HOW TO DISAGREE

ADAM FERNER &
DARREN CHETTY

HOW TO
DISAGREE

NEGOTIATE DIFFERENCE
IN A DIVIDED WORLD.

WHITE LION
PUBLISHING

Brimming with creative inspiration, how-to projects and useful information to enrich your everyday life, Quarto Knows is a favourite destination for those pursuing their interests and passions. Visit our site and dig deeper with our books into your area of interest: Quarto Creates, Quarto Cooks, Quarto Homes, Quarto Lives, Quarto Drives, Quarto Explores, Quarto Gifts or Quarto Kids.

First published in 2019 by White Lion Publishing
an imprint of The Quarto Group
The Old Brewery, 6 Blundell Street
London N7 9BH
United Kingdom

www.QuartoKnows.com

A catalogue record for this book is available from the British Library.

ISBN 978 1 78131 934 5
Ebook ISBN 978 1 78131 935 2
10 9 8 7 6 5 4 3 2 1
2023 2022 2021 2020 2019

Designed and illustrated by Stuart Tolley of Transmission Design

Printed in China

FSC www.fsc.org
MIX
Paper from responsible sources
FSC® C008047

For Nathaniel Adam Tobias ~~Coleman~~

CONTENTS

03 UNDERSTANDING CONFLICT

04 REACHING OUT

05 MOVING FORWARD

INTRODUCTION

Disagreements are a fact of life. They can be difficult, messy and deeply uncomfortable – but they're also profoundly *important*. The discomfort that disagreements can provoke isn't always something to be shied away from – and the messiness we find is often a reflection of the complex nature of our everyday lives. Disagreements can be awkward – they can be exhausting and tough – but that doesn't mean we have to avoid them.

This book isn't designed to make disagreements 'smoother' or more 'palatable', or to dissolve them. We're not going to tell you how to 'win' an argument or outline the neat rhetorical moves for outsmarting and out-styling your opponent. Nor are we going to get into the philosophical nitty-gritty of argumentation, the careful logic by which premises follow one another towards a sound conclusion. And we're not going to suggest good manners are the solution either. There are books that encourage you to disagree 'politely', to doff your cap after every comment and call each other 'Sir' or 'Madam'. When looking at how to disagree, the best tactic is not to pretend that you don't.

The first chapter of the book, 'Me, Myself and I', looks at who we are. When we converse with others, we typically have an idea of ourselves as discrete rational agents. This concept of a unitary self comes from a very particular tradition – and it's not one that everyone buys into. We look at critiques of the 'rational subject', and issues of group agency. We'll also delve into debates about the reality (or lack thereof) of free will and the dependability of truth.

The second chapter, 'Revealing Systems', looks at the frameworks that organize how we interact. We're going to be looking at the ethical puzzles raised by 'codes of conduct' (like good manners) and the notable gaps that exist – by design or otherwise – in our understanding of the world. We'll look at the different ways of engaging with others, through debates and dialogues, and what it means to speak freely.

Chapter three, 'Understanding Conflict', will examine some of the ways we slip up in conversation and the kind of damage that can result. Using the prism of Euro-American epistemology – the branch of philosophy that deals with knowledge – we'll explore how 'panic' functions to bring conversations to a close, and what 'diversionary tactics' are. We'll also look at how 'speaking for others' can present problems, and when might or might not be an appropriate time for action.

'I am totally down with disagreement. I don't like Haterade but disagreement is wonderful. When someone disagrees, we try to reach common ground. That's good.'
Roxane Gay

In chapter four, 'Reaching Out', we'll look at methods for building bridges. How do we express solidarity with others, and what's the value in doing so? Meal-sharing or 'inter-dining' is a particularly interesting way of reaching out – and as we'll see in the section on humour, jokes can play a central role in bringing people together too.

The final chapter is called 'Moving Forward'. All too often, conversations get stuck in ruts; the idea in this part is to examine four different topics – veganism, climate change, euthanasia and white supremacy – as they are embedded in the real world, and to explore strategies for opening them up and shifting them onto different registers; though the final section, 'Self-Care', looks at the importance of knowing when to pause and when to stop completely.

This book is itself the product of a dialogue (and, sometimes, disagreements). While the words you're reading were largely written by Adam, the thoughts they express emerged from long – often exciting, sometimes baffling – conversations, which took place over coffee and Oreos in Darren's front room. We've agreed and disagreed, laughed and scowled about the topics that feature here, and our contents list is a result of deliberation and negotiation with each other and our publishers.

And though we don't necessarily reach any capital-C Conclusions or capital-S Solutions, there is one idea that runs throughout, towards which both of us are profoundly sympathetic: disagreement is essential. Talking, arguing, debating, discussing . . . in the right conditions, these can be incredibly worthwhile activities. They can be even better when they're enjoyed with different people, from different places, with different points of view. So, whether or not you agree with the thoughts found in this book, we hope – at the very least – that they'll provide some good topics for conversation . . .

HOW TO USE THIS BOOK

This book is organized into five parts and 20 sections covering the ways we can navigate productive disagreement.

BUILD + BECOME

Each section introduces you to an important concept,

BUILD + **BECOME**

and explains how you can apply what you've learned to everyday life.

As you go through the book, TOOLKITS help you keep track of what you've learned so far.

Specially curated FURTHER LEARNING notes give you a nudge in the right direction for those things that most captured your imagination.

At BUILD+BECOME we believe in building knowledge that helps you navigate your world. So, dip in, take it step-by-step, or digest it all in one go — however you choose to read this book, enjoy and get thinking.

PRODUCTIV
DISAGREEM
ARE PROFO
IMPORTANT

E
ENTS
UNDLY

ME, MYSELF AND I

SECTIONS

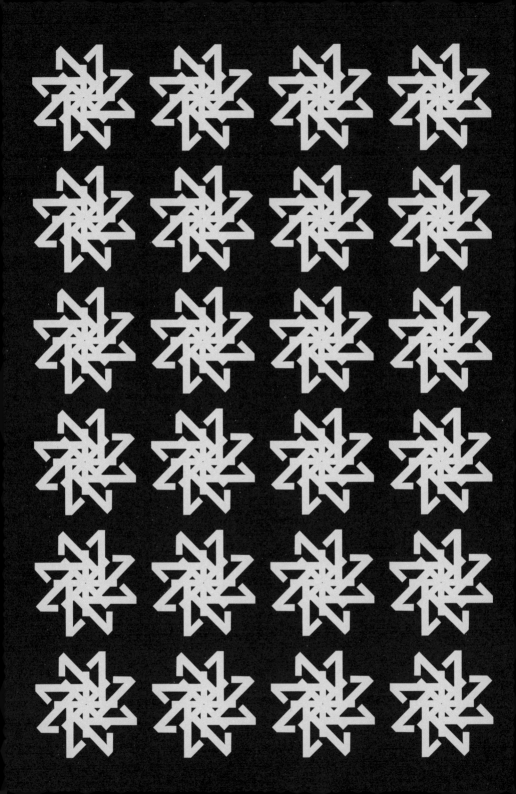

'We can disagree and still love each other, unless your disagreement is rooted in my oppression and denial of my humanity and right to exist.'
James Baldwin

What kinds of things get into arguments? *Argumentative* things, sure – but more broadly? Things like us. Humans. People. Individuals. In this chapter, we're going to focus on 'metaphysics' – the area of philosophy that examines the nature of reality. We're going to investigate the metaphysical character of these special entities who get into fights, converse, engage in dialogue and debate. We're going to look at their nature, and how they exist in the world.

For thousands of years, philosophers have been putting forward stories about the kinds of beings we are. Whether they construe us as essentially 'thinking things' or 'embodied consciousnesses', every story moderates the ways in which we interact with each other. One account, popular since the seventeenth century, holds that we are 'rational subjects' – boundaried, self-governing intelligences who are privy to our own thoughts and nobody else's. In section 1, 'Being Me', we're going to examine this seemingly intuitive notion. Are our thoughts really so discrete? There are certainly some situations – like the co-authored text you're currently reading – which suggest that the reality is more complex.

We're also going to look at the larger entities – groups, communities, societies in general – that these human individuals make up. In section 2, 'Group Chat', we're going to think about 'group agency' and what it means for a group to have a 'will'. How does social power *move through* individuals? Can the 'will' of a society shape the actions of its citizens?

In the third section, 'Free Thinking', we're going to look at agency more generally. When we engage in dialogue, we typically do so on the understanding that each of us has the power to change minds – our own and other people's. This understanding rests on metaphysical assumptions about 'free will'. How realistic is it to think we can transcend the effects of our backgrounds? Is it impossible for us to escape the causal chains that precede us?

The final section, 'Hard Facts', deals with a philosophical concept that's frequently and often problematically invoked in daily discourse: truth. Arguments are normally arbitrated by reference to what's 'true' or 'false', 'fact' or 'fiction', 'objective' or 'subjective', and these ideas are all connected to specific conceptions of reality. Are there really external facts, which we can point to in order to decide who's right or wrong, or is everything just relative?

This chapter attempts to show that our appeals to facts, or our ideas about free will, are grounded in long-running metaphysical debates. Whenever you say something's 'true', or argue for the 'freedom to choose', you're assuming something about the structure of the world, about the way reality actually, genuinely is. The aim here is to bring these assumptions to light to see how they affect the ways we engage with one another.

BEING ME

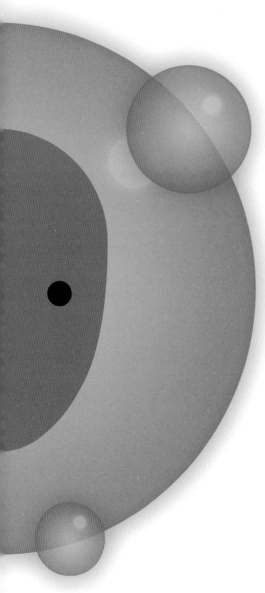

'If I were you . . .'
'But you're not! You don't get it! You don't know what it's like!'

Words are wonderful, but at the end of the day they only go so far. There are some thoughts, feelings and lived experiences that are almost, if not actually, impossible to communicate. In the exchange above, we see how this features in our everyday disagreements.

At the heart of such claims is the thought that I am distinct from you, and that there are certain things, desires and opinions that exist in the privacy of my head and are inaccessible to you.

This idea, that we are discrete 'rational subjects', cordoned off from the world, transfuses our daily lives and our politics. For instance, it underpins our democratic voting procedures: every member of society has their personal view (about who should be elected) and communicates it with a cross in a box or the raising of an arm. It's the idea of a rational subject that makes sense of opinion polls and surveys, which ask what people think (because only they themselves know). It's this notion that causes us to bristle when others claim to have greater insight into our views than we do ourselves. We might say: 'No one knows me better than I know myself.'

This seems a perfectly ordinary, almost natural way of looking at the world. But while there may well be features of human experience that *inform* the idea of a 'rational subject' (like our experience of the privacy of our personal thoughts), the American philosopher Amélie Oksenberg Rorty points out that human experience has historically been theorized in different ways. The rational subject is just one of these ways and a product of a particular socio-political context.

The idea of a discrete, closed-off, thinking thing emerged during the period known as the Western Enlightenment or (in a similarly self-congratulatory vein) The Age of Reason. During the seventeenth and eighteenth centuries, philosophers like René Descartes, John Locke and Jean-Jacques Rousseau contributed to what is now a hugely influential picture of personhood. They introduced the idea of the *boundaried* nature of our selves, along with our capacity for reason. So we find in Descartes' *Meditations* (1641) the idea of a rational subject so far removed from others it can come to doubt its very existence. In his famous argument, *'Cogito ergo sum'* ('I think therefore I am'), Descartes posits the existence of a thinking being who can only really be sure of its own existence. It knows itself, but not others.

The German philosopher Immanuel Kant also contributes to this train of thought. In *Critique of Pure Reason* (1781), Kant argues that reason is a special capacity, possessed by each individual, which allows us to arbitrate the truth of judgements – and thereby reach decisions for ourselves. Reason allows us to 'self-govern', or act 'autonomously'.

The rational subject is not a natural concept. Nor is it a metaphysical whimsy. It emerged in response to institutional abuses by ruling powers of the time, like the Church and the monarchy. The rational subject is understood by Kant to have ownership of its own thoughts, to possess opinions, and to be able to appeal to reason just as well as any king or bishop.

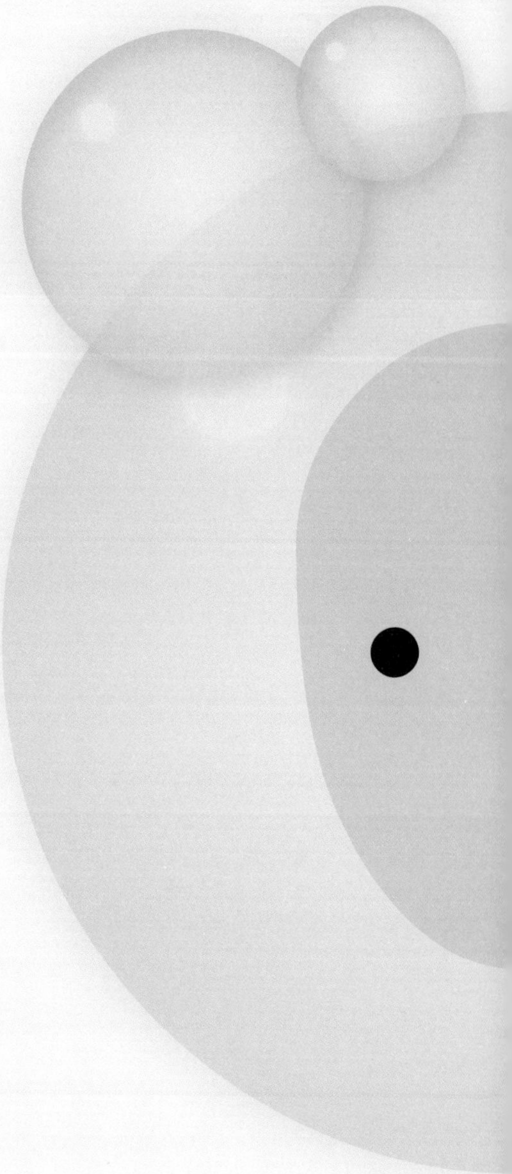

NO 'I' IN TEAM

The rational subject gained so much theoretical traction during the Age of Reason that it was reified – *made real* – and figures prominently in metaphysical systems of the time (the philosophical accounts of the structure of reality). Modern thinkers like Kant and Descartes held that along with material things (like particles) and qualities (like colours), there are these thinking things too – selves, or persons.

However, in becoming a more substantial entity, the politics of the rational subject was unhelpfully obscured. That, at least, is the contention of the Critical Theorists. Based in Frankfurt, and known not-so-imaginatively as the Frankfurt School, twentieth-century thinkers like Theodor Adorno, Max Horkheimer and Herbert Marcuse critique the seemingly common-sensical notion of a discrete thinking thing.

Marcuse, for example, sees the rational subject as an essential part of the economic system known as capitalism (in which private owners employ others in order to make profit in the marketplace). In *One-Dimensional Man* (1964), he argues that the notion of a distinct, self-governing individual – a manageable body, who can labour and perform discrete tasks – is a socioeconomic necessity of market capitalism. Here, rational subjects are the building blocks out of which a capitalist economy is constructed.

Postmodern and feminist scholars have revealed other hidden – and troubling – features of the rational subject. This idea of subjecthood is grounded in a specific notion of reason, which appears to be constructed to disenfranchise certain groups of people. One of the 'great luminaries' of the Enlightenment, Kant promoted a conception of reason that was indelibly bound up with his profound racism. In 'The Color of Reason' (1997), Emmanuel Chukwudi Eze examines texts such as Kant's 'On the Different Races of Man' (1775), in which Kant positions white Europeans at the top of a racial hierarchy. Eze points out that the notion of the 'universal human subject' is, for Kant, a white European man. Similarly, feminist scholars like Genevieve Lloyd and Rae Langton have drawn attention to the way Kant's 'reason' is bound up with his corrosive sexism. His approach to 'intellectual women' was horrendously dismissive – saying they 'might as well even have a beard'. As formulated by Kant and his Enlightenment friends, reason is implicitly 'gendered'. It's understood to be masculine – a capacity possessed by men (with beards).

It's important, therefore, to recognize the context from which our self-conception emerges. While ideally the 'rational subject' is a position that's democratically open to all – bishop and peasant alike – in reality it carries with it assumptions about gender, race and class (among others).

'Reason' has a history. Whether we like it or not, this history can inform our ideas about who is and isn't a rational subject. It bubbles to the surface when, for instance, women are accused of being emotional, hysterical or irrational. And it can shape how we perceive our conversation partner and how we respond to them.

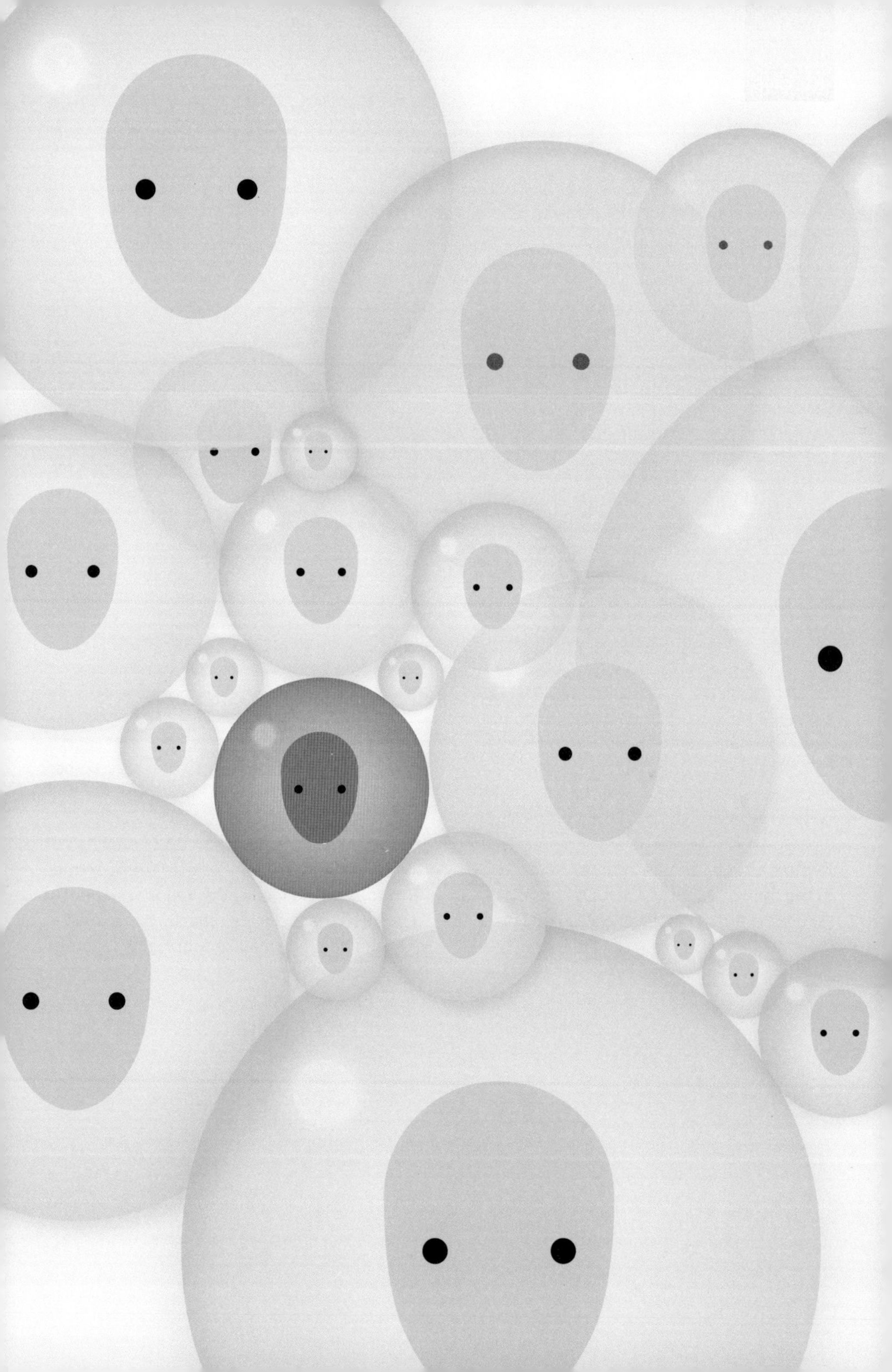

GROUP CHAT

In 2016, the British public was asked to vote on whether or not to leave the European Union. The result – 48.1 per cent of voters backed 'remain'; 51.9 per cent backed 'leave' – came to be known as 'Brexit', the British Exit from the EU. After the referendum, Prime Minister Theresa May – who was charged with upholding the result – said repeatedly that she was enacting 'the will of the people'. This phrase made many uncomfortable, especially those whose desires were not reflected in the outcome. This is a discomfort we sometimes feel when it comes to the phenomenon known as 'group agency'.

Individual agency seems pretty straightforward. Individuals have control over their own actions and unless coerced or otherwise constrained, they can do whatever they choose to do. Occasionally, however, individual agents come together, and through a process of joint deliberation they can enact things *together* – like leaving a union of nation states. The group acts as an individual agent. As the Brexit vote demonstrates, however, such group actions can be highly confusing. If a people has a 'will', where is it located? What kind of force is it?

The idea of 'a general will' is found in canonical form in the work of the eighteenth-century French philosopher Jean-Jacques Rousseau. In his book, *The Social Contract* (1762), Rousseau distinguishes between 'particular will', which focuses on the interests of an individual (your desire for an ice-cream), and 'general will', which focuses on communal interests (the public 'desire' for something like a National Health Service). For Rousseau, 'As long as several men assembled together consider themselves as a single body, they have only *one will* which is directed towards their common preservation and general well-being.' This general will is manifest in the result of a vote.

It's a popular and influential thought, but not without its critics. Among them

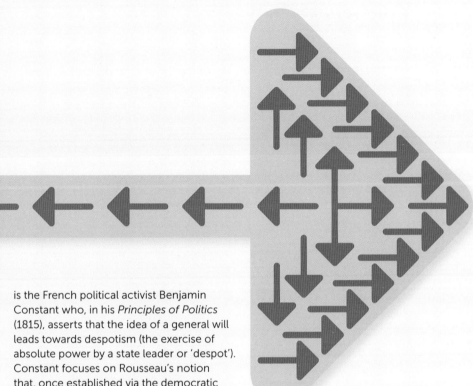

is the French political activist Benjamin Constant who, in his *Principles of Politics* (1815), asserts that the idea of a general will leads towards despotism (the exercise of absolute power by a state leader or 'despot'). Constant focuses on Rousseau's notion that, once established via the democratic process, the general will becomes *unimpeachable*. The members of the group have to submit to it completely, to the point where those who voted against it must admit to having been in error.

Constant saw this political model as open to grave misuse by those in power. What if the means by which the group determines the general will is dodgy? What if the self-appointed 'representatives of the people' are dodgy too? According to Constant, Rousseau's theory leads us to surrender ourselves 'to those who act in the name of all'. Politicians who put themselves forward as 'the voice of the people' might, in reality, be anything but.

'WHAT'S THE RATIONALE?'

Making group decisions is difficult, clearly. 'You can't please everyone' is almost a truism when public opinion about policy is so dramatically divided. And it's a difficulty that occurs at every level – international, national and local. Whether it's in a polity or a business, a multinational company or a freelance partnership, *people disagree*.

There are methods, however, for making group deliberation easier and more effective. In his *Theory of Justice* (1971), the political theorist John Rawls emphasizes the importance of recognizing different forms of 'practical reasoning'. What, he asks, is the framework within which our group deliberation takes place? Or put another way, how should we engage in the democratic process? Settling such questions allows us to deliberate together more carefully.

PLURALISTS

For 'pluralists', democracy (from the Greek *demos*, 'people', and -*cracy*, 'rule') is a matter of group members basing their decisions on private interests. There is a *plurality* of individual concerns and everyone votes with their own particular issues in mind. This can involve teaming up with people who share the same interests – but it needn't. For the pluralists, there's no call for group members to engage with each other except insofar as they might further their own individual interests.

This is a mercenary approach to group deliberation. It neglects something we call 'the common good'.

COMMON GOOD

The common good can be understood as encompassing communal interests (an educated public, say, or a pleasant work environment) and facilities (state-owned libraries or, on a smaller level, an office biscuit tin). Political philosophers from Aristotle onwards have argued that the common good should be the primary focus of deliberative democracy. When we vote as a group, we should vote with *everyone's* interests in mind, not just our own. Not doing so is seen to be a weakness of the pluralists' position.

As Rawls points out, we use different forms of 'practical reasoning' in different contexts. In a market context, for instance, managers make decisions based on what's best for the company's finances, which might have unfortunate consequences for competitors. In such cases, 'our' interests are prioritized over 'theirs'. Yet Rawls believes this isn't how people are typically supposed to reason in an ideal democracy. We see some acknowledgment of this in the fact that political parties don't explicitly press for legislation that disadvantages certain social groups over others.

So how do you participate in group decisions? As a cut-throat business person working in a competitive field you may be looking out for Number One (yourself). Here, your contribution is probably informed by a *pluralistic* rationale. What about when you vote as a member of society – in a national election, for instance? Instead of being motivated by self-interest, your voting may well be directed towards the provision of 'common goods'.

We can engage in group decisions in different ways. One thing that's important to remember, however, is that the group decision, the 'general will', will likely be more comprehensible if we understand the *rationale* behind each individual's engagement. Think about your last argument: did you disagree about the rationale or about how best to achieve the stated aims?

IF THE PEO
'WILL', WH
LOCATED?

PLE HAVE A
ERE IS IT

FREE THINKING

Imagine you're chatting with your granddad and he says something transphobic. Later on, your mum excuses him, saying, 'He's a product of his time'. She might even say, 'He can't help it, it's how he was brought up'.

In saying this, your mum is invoking the metaphysical thesis known as 'determinism'. Occasionally called 'causal determinism', it holds that all events are completely and utterly fixed – or determined – by earlier events. It's an intuitive position. We know the world works according to specific physical laws and that things are causally connected and result from prior events. So we can assume that, with sufficient information, we could (theoretically) work out what the effect of all our actions would be. This would include people's behaviour. Granddad's transphobia may be the direct and inevitable consequence of his growing up in a transphobic society, just as your fear of dogs may be an inevitable consequence of your having been bitten by a dog when you were little. It makes sense. Cause. Effect.

Of course, with our limited understanding of the world, we may never be able to actually predict the future. But it's possible, in principle, and that's all your mum needs in order to absolve your granddad. It's not his fault, he's just a product of his time.

There are other ways of putting distance between ourselves and our actions. We often talk about being caught up in the 'zeitgeist' or the 'spirit of an age'. These phrases are borne from the philosophical tradition known as 'Historicism', popular among German philosophers in the eighteenth century. Historicism holds that our actions are expressions of a cosmic will. The German thinker Georg Wilhelm Friedrich Hegel believes that individual actions are manifestations of this 'world soul', or universal 'spirit' *(geist)*.

Weird, right? Most of the time we tend to think we're in charge of our destinies rather than puppets of some omniscient deity, or *geist*, or outputs of the plodding mechanics of the physical universe. This type of deterministic thinking is at odds with how we engage with each other in arguments and conversations. We think we can persuade people – and be persuaded – with arguments (and perhaps a sprinkling of rhetoric). We think we can reach into a seemingly deterministic world and exert control over ourselves and others.

Are we deluded? Have a think. When was the last time you changed your mind during a conversation – or someone else changed their opinion because of something you said? How many of your beliefs have you managed to actively reassess and relinquish since they were formed in your childhood?

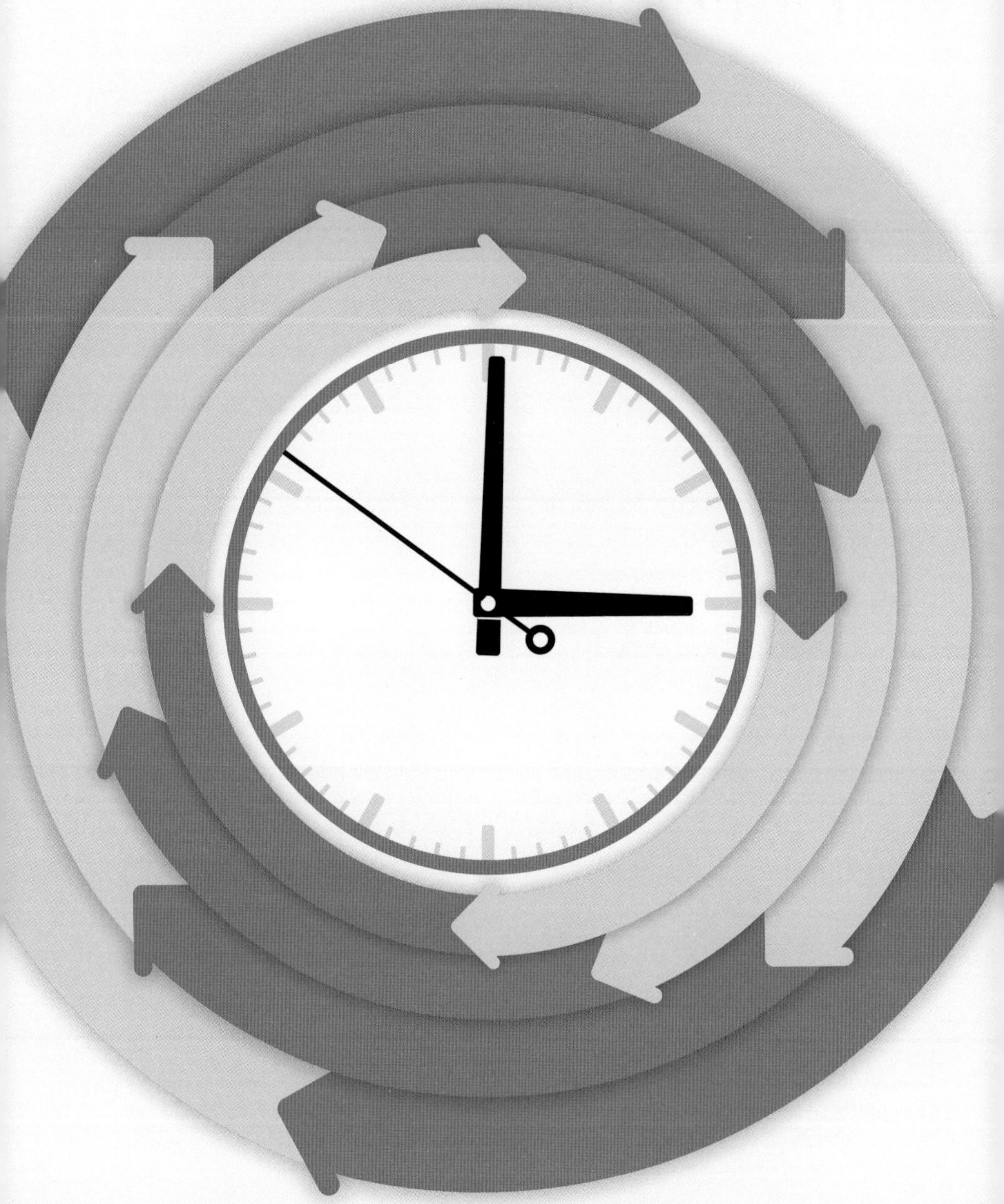

'THINK FOR YOURSELF'

Are our characters set in stone from the moment of birth? Working at the start of the nineteenth century, 'Romantics' like Friedrich Wilhelm Joseph von Schelling thought our understanding of ourselves was the result of a process of self-discovery. Through self-investigation, introspection and exposure to certain meaningful encounters (awe-inspiring things like seascapes and mountain ranges), we find ourselves. There is, Schelling thought, some true essence that makes you you. You may be a hero or a coward, a villain or a saint – whatever it is, there's some inner-core baked into you, waiting to be discovered.

This idea nicely complements the deterministic worldview – but it's not quite as fatalistic as some forms of 'hard determinism'. Life for the Romantics doesn't just unfold joylessly according to a cosmic blueprint. The Romantic is a 'compatibilist', who holds that determinism is compatible with a degree of freedom. Sure, they say, the self might be there already, fixed by nature, but that doesn't mean we don't have a role to play. It's up to us to find out what we are. And it's up to us to act according to, and to cultivate, our true nature. We can be free, they say, in the way a river may be free to run its course, or a balloon, once released, is free to soar up up up.

In contrast to the Romantics, 'Existentialists' – like Simone de Beauvoir, Jean-Paul Sartre and Frantz Fanon – thought compatibilism was an impoverished form of freedom. Working in the twentieth century, these thinkers focused less on self-discovery and more on self-creation. Their mantra was 'Existence precedes essence'. You come into existence then decide how to exist. You decide what to exist as, who to be. In its most radical form, existentialism holds that you are utterly unconstrained by your upbringing. You can break free, completely, from the causal chains that brought you into the world.

If these positions – the Romantic and Existentialist – strike you as too extreme, you'll be relieved to learn there are philosophers who tread the line between the two. The philosopher and cultural theorist Kwame Anthony Appiah is one. He recognizes the importance of acknowledging the circumstances you're born into, the capacities you enjoy and the privations you suffer, but he also denies that we have to be determined by these facts. In defining ourselves, he says we engage in creative acts of self-construction: 'To create a life is to create a life out of the materials that history has given you.'

Seyla Benhabib, a professor of philosophy at Yale, toes a similar line. We are not merely extensions of causal chains, she says. We 'are in the position of author and character at once'. Our identity is not just a matter of pre-made artefact nor of spontaneous generation. It's a creative combination of the two.

There's a common thread that connects these varied thoughts about free will. Agency, in any form, requires effort; there is an imperative to engage. If you don't, if you sit back and fail to examine yourself, you'll end up as a passive extension of a causal chain – a product of your time. Conversation is a crucial element of these self-revelations. The back-and-forth with others allows you to get a better sense of your own boundaries, your own interests, and the things you can and cannot change about yourself.

HARD FACTS

Imagine a world where everyone lies. You ask someone the time and they tell you it's noon when it's midnight. You ask for directions and you're told to go left instead of right. What kind of world would this be? A highly dysfunctional one. When we talk to each other, we rely on our partners telling the truth.

But what is truth, exactly? One widespread view states that claims about truth and falsity rely on the assumption that there's a real, external world that exists independently of how we conceive it. Statements that grass is green, or water is composed of hydrogen and oxygen molecules, are true – they're *facts* – if they accurately map these features of the external world.

For the 'realist', the world can meet our expectations or it can frustrate them. It does so irrespective of what we think about it. The molecular composition of water is not a matter of opinion (it's not 'subjective'); reality has the final say (it's 'objective').

Of course, there are different kinds of facts, and different domains where 'truth' and 'falsity' appear to apply. Some are more contentious than others. Scientific facts seem relatively straightforward. Through empirical investigation (via your senses) you can work out, for instance, that humans need water to survive. That's a fact that's hard to dispute without risking dehydration. But what about facts in other spheres? Is there a fact of the matter about whether an artwork is beautiful? The 'Mona Lisa' isn't everyone's cup of tea.

And what about morality? Are there moral facts floating about in the external world? Do you think, as 'moral realists' like Plato did, that we can discover objective moral truths – like the fact that the killing of innocents is always wrong – in the same way that we can discover facts about the molecular composition of water?

The concepts of *truth, objectivity* and *fact* can be confusing. 'Postmodernists' like Judith Butler and Bruno Latour have shown that they can also be politically fraught. They critique what they see to be the idea of Universal Truth that emerged during 'Modernism' (the European intellectual milieu of the nineteenth and twentieth centuries), and show how the idea of objectivity has been historically used as a tool of oppression. Social bodies like the state or the scientific establishment can declare that they have neutral access to what is *really* the case – when in fact they don't. 'Facts', say the postmodernists, 'are not discovered, but made'; created by certain people in order to control others. The racist views that underpinned the transatlantic slave trade were couched as objective fact, just as homosexuality was medically pathologized in the early twentieth century.

Given the way claims to objectivity and truth can be abused, perhaps it's best to just declare that 'Everything's relative!' 'It's all just a matter of opinion!' This appears to be the direction that the postmodernists are leading us in. But this approach has its problems too.

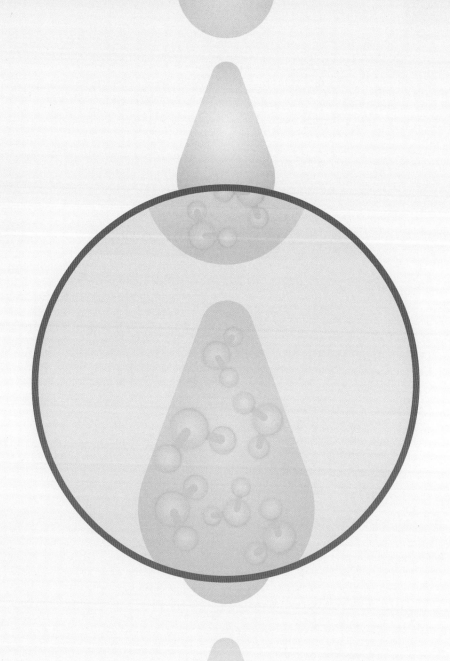

'THE POST-TRUTH ERA'

If you're not a realist, you may be a relativist. For the relativist, things like truth, goodness and beauty are *relative* to some frame of reference – and there are no absolute standards with which to judge between these competing frames. For instance, an act that's considered polite in one culture (collecting mucus in a small towel known as a 'handkerchief') may be seen as distasteful in another. Or something that's deemed morally acceptable in some countries (eating the flesh of dead animals) may be deemed intolerable in others. The boiling point of water is normally taken to be 100 degrees Celsius, but in certain situations (when dissolved oxygen is removed, say) it can be very different. It's all relative to the frame of reference – the culture, the background conditions – and there's no over-arching framework that allows us to say one system is better than another.

As the philosopher Gopal Sreenivasan points out, a touch of relativism is helpful in multicultural societies where we live alongside people with vastly different cultural and religious perspectives. At the same time, it has certain drawbacks because appeals to truth and objective facts help us resist being controlled by unjust forces.

The thought that truth is in some way essential to our ability to protect ourselves from injustice is found in the work of the political theorist Hannah Arendt. In her 1951 book, *The Origins of Totalitarianism*, Arendt connects the blurring of fact and fiction with the rise of totalitarianism. According to Arendt, the threat of totalitarianism arises because facts constitute fixed external points with which individuals can settle disputes. If we no longer know what's true and false, if we start acknowledging what we now call 'alternative facts', it's much easier for those in power to exert their control over us.

Say, for instance, that you and I are arguing over whether or not water is composed of hydrogen and oxygen molecules. There's a 'fact of the matter', here. It's something we can go and check in a laboratory. Water is composed of hydrogen and oxygen (H_2O), so the disagreement can be resolved. Imagine, however, that someone comes along and says that all chemists are untrustworthy, that molecular science is a scam. We'd be presented with 'alternative facts', emerging from an alternative body of knowledge. Depending on how much credence we give this person, and this 'knowledge', the line between what's true and false would blur.

Arendt thinks this blurring deprives democratic societies of external points of purchase. The power to arbitrate disputes, to decide who's right, comes to be wielded by those with the most power and the loudest voices (often the leaders of the state).

The postmodernists show us how concepts like 'objectivity' and 'truth' are used to oppress marginalized groups. It was 'objective' Western science, for example, that claimed that women were less intelligent than men. Arendt argues that those same concepts are essential for us to resist those same oppressive forces; science provides us with reliable, objective evidence that allows us to challenge the sexist and misogynistic views of patriarchal societies.

It may just be a matter of opinion. But wherever you finally fall, the truth is that the truth is clearly important for *everyone*. Whether you think truth is relative, or hard-and-fast, will affect how you converse with others.

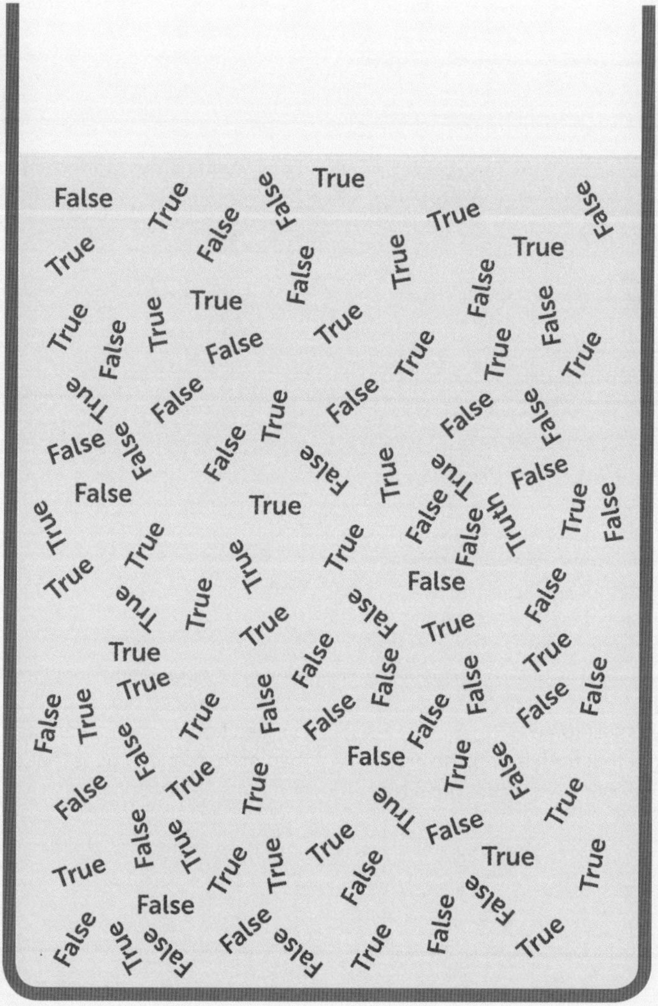
False
True
False
False
True
True
False
True
False
True
True
False
True
False
True
True
False
True
True
False
True
True
True
False
True
False
False
False
False
False
False
False
True
True
False
False
True
False
False
Truth
True
False
True
True
True
True
True
False
True
True
False
False
True
True
True
False
True
False
True
False
True
True
False
False
False
False
False
False
False
False
False
True
False
False
True
True
True
False
True
True
False
True
True
True
True
True
True
True
False
False
False
True
False
False
False
True
False
False
True

BUILD +
BECOME

TOOLKIT

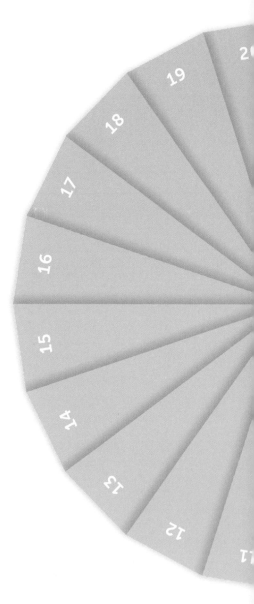

01

Historically, the concept of rationality positions some subjects as more 'rational' than others. During disagreements, consider whether you and your interlocutor see each other as 'irrational'. Are these views grounded in the *argument* or in how you're *behaving*?

02

We typically think that groups, such as political parties, possess a 'general will'. We tend to think they can form decisions and perform group actions. When arguing, do you see your partner as an *individual* or *a representative of a group*? Ask them how they perceive you.

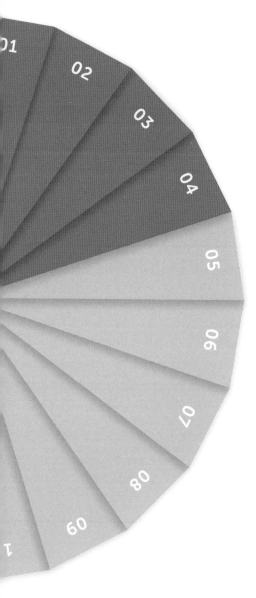

03

Some people believe we're just 'products of our environment' and as such completely causally determined. While it's helpful to recognize how attitudes emerge from specific belief systems, the view that someone *necessarily* thinks certain things creates obstacles to conversation.

04

People often disagree about what is and isn't 'true'. Relativists, however, say that 'truth' is simply the opinion of the dominant group. When arguing, do you believe what you're saying is true for everyone, or 'true for *you*'?

FURTHER LEARNING

READ

'Descartes Was Wrong'
Abeba Birhane (Aeon, 2017)

Grand Hotel Abyss
Stuart Jeffries (Verso, 2016)

thinkingspace.org.uk
Grace Lockrobin

WATCH

Philosophy TV is a website where top philosophers beam in from around the world to disagree with each other: philostv.com

LISTEN

'Conversations With People Who Hate Me' podcasts. Dylan Marron frequently receives hate mail in response to his online videos. In these podcasts, he calls up and speaks to those who post negative messages.

VISIT

A governmental debate. As is the case in many countries, UK citizens and international visitors can watch politicians discuss legislation (in the House of Commons or House of Lords). Similarly, in the US visitors can visit Congress and see political debate in action.

REVEALING SYSTEMS

SECTIONS

'It is the nature of privilege to find ever deeper places to hide.'
Elizabeth Spelman

Humans are social creatures. We hang out. We talk. We shoot the breeze. Over the course of our evolution we've developed an impressive variety of ways to communicate with one another. We have systems that help us to reach out, to convey to friends, families, work colleagues and strangers our innermost thoughts.

As well as multifarious digital technologies – texts, emails and more – we have tried and tested social conventions that help us talk to each other. We have an idea of the things that help and hinder good conversation. Shouting and screaming are conversational no-nos. The ideal conversationalist is calm, polite and courteous. We have systems and these systems work. Or so we tell ourselves.

The aim of this chapter is to examine these conversational systems in greater depth. What are the background ideas organizing them? What are the social attitudes and assumptions that structure our exchanges?

It's clear from even a cursory survey of the news that while society aspires to 'free and open debate', some people are allowed to speak more freely and openly than others. Some voices ring louder and carry further. In section 5, 'Speaking Freely', we look at the celebrated notion of 'free speech' and examine how it applies to different people in different contexts. Is it really as 'egalitarian' as we assume? Does everyone have an equal opportunity to speak freely? The brief answer is no, probably not.

Section 6, 'Political Politeness', focuses on what appears to be an unproblematic conversational virtue: politeness. Surely it's good to be polite to each other? There's never any need for rudeness . . . right? In this section we follow philosophers like bell hooks and Mary Wollstonecraft and examine the idea that politeness is a profoundly political concept, often used to empower some speakers and silence others.

What are arguments exactly? This is the framing question for section 7, 'Argument, Debate and Dialogue'. Often, arguments are portrayed as fights. We examine the benefits of engaging in combative arguments and explore some alternatives.

In the final section, 'Ignorance', we look at how gaps appear in our understanding of the world. Ignorance is often understood as a passive phenomenon – an absence, a void, a simple lack of knowledge – but here we wonder whether it is, instead, an intentional, active system for suppressing certain perspectives and perpetuating unjust institutions. Is ignorance bliss? And if so, for whom?

Humans are social creatures. But we're fallible too, and prone to confusion. It may well be that our methods of communication are not quite as helpful, nor as efficient or fair, as we would like to imagine. This chapter will look at where these broken systems may need fixing.

SPEAKING FREELY

'You can't say that!'
'Free speech' is highly valued in democratic societies. We like being able to speak our minds without being told to shut up. It's a sign of a healthy democracy if citizens are encouraged to communicate their thoughts and beliefs – and a sign of an oppressive political system if speech is restricted.

Despite our valuing free speech, however, it may sometimes feel necessary to place limits on what people can say. Unfortunately, it's not always clear when it's appropriate to do so. Is it okay to shush someone who's talking during a film screening? What about a toddler shouting in the quiet carriage? Or when you hear someone saying something homophobic or inciting violence?

The guide employed by most societies is something called 'the Harm principle'. We find a classic formulation of this in John Stuart Mill's *On Liberty* (1859): 'The only purpose for which power can be rightfully exercised over any member of a civilized community, against his will, is to prevent harm to others.'

The Harm principle allows us to intervene, for instance, if a speaker intends to stir up religious hatred. Speech that incites violence against a religious group is necessarily harmful and should therefore be stopped.

A lot of debate here turns on what is and what isn't considered 'harmful'. Some philosophers have a wider view that encompasses symbolic harm – the perpetuation of offensive stereotypes, say. Others have a narrower conception, focusing primarily on physical harm; a 'speech act' is harmful if it constitutes a direct physical threat to another's safety. Those with this

narrower conception are sometimes referred to as 'Libertarians', because they think speech should be as free and unencumbered as possible. We should, they say, be at *liberty* to say what we like.

In opposing what they see as 'over-regulation' of speech, Libertarians sometimes make reference to the 'marketplace of ideas'. They argue that the ideal society is one in which we're exposed to as many ideas as possible, and free to 'buy' the ones we find compelling, without paternalistic influence. To limit the ideas on offer (to shut people up) would require someone else – usually the government – to decide which ideas we should be exposed to, and there's no good reason to think they are better placed to decide than we are.

Libertarians appear interestingly optimistic here. There's an assumption that regulation is unnecessary because people gravitate towards progressive, socially convivial ideas while rejecting regressive, hateful ones. But do the best ideas always 'win'? And whose ideas are they anyway?

Let's extend the metaphor of the marketplace. All around the world, independent retailers are being replaced by supermarkets. These supermarkets offer a wide variety of goods but little locally farmed produce. As a result, local businesses have fewer outlets, and in some cases fail. The marketplace of ideas is bustling – but the ideas on sale are not necessarily ones from 'local' minority perspectives. What if minority perspectives don't 'sell'? As in supermarkets, some items are promoted over others, and there's a very real risk that in Libertarian discussions, the interests of marginalized people will be excluded.

SPEAK YOUR MIND

Harmful statements are one thing, but what about harmful questions? Are there some things that just shouldn't be 'up for debate'? Imagine someone wanting to discuss whether a certain group of people should be accorded human rights – should we allow them to do so? Is there any harm in simply 'entertaining the question'?

The Libertarian would allow such a person to raise almost any issue, probably with the aim of exposing the errors in their thinking. *The truth will out* (or so they claim). Critics of Libertarianism, however, worry that people are often committed to their views, irrespective of evidence to the contrary. We've all had debates where participants refuse to change their minds, stubbornly ignoring relevant facts or arguments.

What if, by taking part in a public debate – on the television or at a university campus – troubling, dehumanizing views end up being broadcast to larger and larger audiences? This kind of signal boosting affects a shift in something called 'the Overton window'. Named after the American political scientist Joseph Overton, the 'window' encapsulates the set of ideas tolerated in public discourse. The raising of bigoted opinions in public settings suggests to audiences that they're not only *worthy* of public discourse but, by association, reasonable grounds for public policy.

Think as well about the effects such discussions have on the groups whose humanity is being called into question. Philosophers from Frantz Fanon to Simone de Beauvoir have documented the pervasive emotional and psychological traumas that have historically resulted from these debates on people of colour and women.

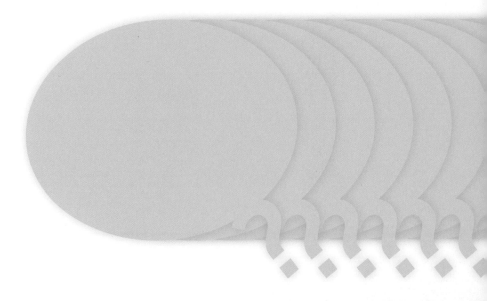

Philosophers like Shelley Tremain and Elizabeth Barnes have demonstrated how the same kinds of questions harm disabled people.

Think too of the difficulties faced by someone from this group in entering the supposedly egalitarian 'marketplace of ideas'. They are already in a marginalized position – lacking access to media and funding – so it will take considerable effort for them to get their views heard. And even if they're not utterly exhausted by the debate, they will, as the scholar-activist Audre Lorde points out, be taken away from pursuing other projects: 'There is a constant drain of energy which might be better used in redefining ourselves and devising realistic scenarios for altering the present and constructing the future.'

Here, it seems the Libertarian's notion of an open forum, where all ideas can be voiced and heard equally well, does not stand up to scrutiny. With this in mind, you may well be persuaded (in certain circumstances) to defend the practice known as 'no-platforming'. No-platforming, or 'deplatforming', is a form of boycott where an organization makes the decision to not give a platform to certain speakers. Libertarians like Jonathan Haidt suggest that this practice leads to an environment in which individuals are unnecessarily sheltered from challenging arguments. By contrast, Moira Weigel argues that no-platforming is essential for protecting oppressed people from the symbolic and emotional violence of dominant groups.

Are some discussions too harmful to have? Should some voices be silenced? Wherever you land on these questions, the much-vaunted principle of free speech is clearly more controversial than it first seemed.

POLITICAL POLITENESS

We're often told that when conversing with others it's important to be polite. To mind our Ps and Qs (whatever they are). Politeness, it's thought, is necessary for productive dialogue. To be polite is to abide by a seemingly common-sensical code of conduct. Don't swear. Don't throw food. Don't fall asleep. This code, which encourages us to listen, for instance, and not to talk over someone else, facilitates understanding – in contrast to shouting, or talking with our mouths full, which typically put a stop to conversation (or at least severely restrict it).

And politeness opens conversations up. Cultural historians have pointed to the way the idea of politeness came to prominence in the early eighteenth century, replacing the British norm of *decorum* – where people

behaved (decorously) according to their station. Certain types of behaviour were appropriate for certain classes of people. Unlike decorum, 'politesse' is an apparently democratic principle. As the French novelist Madeleine de Scudéry puts it, it 'is wanting not to be the *tyrant* of conversation'. That is, politeness is a way of letting everyone's voice be heard, of everyone 'getting a turn to speak'.

So politeness seems like an unproblematic conversational virtue, right? Not everyone thinks so. The eighteenth-century philosopher Mary Wollstonecraft dismissed politeness as little more than a screen for hypocrisy and egotism. Etymologically, 'polite' shares a root with the word 'polish', and suggests a superficial smoothness – a surface-

level sheen. It's easy to sympathize with Wollstonecraft's view; all too often we find ourselves in situations where insults or barbed comments are smuggled into a conversation masked by a thin veneer of politeness. Some compliments, for instance, can seem polite, encouraging even, while actually being incredibly passive-aggressive. 'Congratulations! I didn't think you'd get that promotion!'

Politeness is examined from another angle by the American philosopher bell hooks, who argues that what counts as 'polite' is primarily, and problematically, determined by 'bourgeois' values. hooks focuses on how politeness plays out in the classroom: in her essay, 'Confronting Class in the Classroom' (1994), she describes how access to 'good manners'

privileges some students and leads to the exclusion of others. 'Loudness, anger, emotional outbursts, and even something as seemingly innocent as unrestrained laughter were deemed unacceptable, vulgar disruptions of classroom social order. These traits were also associated with being a member of the lower classes . . . It is still necessary for students to assimilate bourgeois values in order to be deemed acceptable.'

Is politeness a virtue? Does it oil the otherwise gritty gears of social interactions and promote social harmony? Or is it a mask for the hypocritical to hide behind? Are injunctions to 'speak when spoken to' nothing more than assertions of dominance and control? What are you really objecting to when you call someone 'rude'?

HOW DARE YOU!

The American linguist Robin Lakoff wrote in her essay 'The Logic of Politeness' (1973) that polite behaviour was informed by three maxims: Don't impose; Give options; Make your receiver feel good. Subsequent theorists have expanded these maxims, showing how 'behaving politely' can involve exaggerating one's interest or sympathy, avoiding disagreement, and giving undue deference. These are familiar conversational strategies: nodding earnestly at something you don't understand, biting your tongue to avoid controversy, or allowing someone to talk over you. They're tried and tested methods for a smooth conversation and ultimately (we're told) an easy life.

Unfortunately, while observing these maxims may help preserve the social equilibrium and prevent emotions from running high, they don't necessarily foster honesty. Politeness may ensure that conversations run smoothly, but it privileges good social relations over truth. Worried about this, some philosophers of education suggest that productive dialogue necessarily involves a certain amount of friction. There are certain subjects, they say, which make us feel awkward, and the discomfort we experience is a sign that we're getting close to subjects that matter.

To such philosophers, like Megan Boler, it's not irrelevant that Socrates was described in Plato's *Apology* as a 'gadfly' – buzzing around, stinging his interlocutors into conversational frenzies. He wasn't interested in making them feel at ease.

Following Socrates' example, Boler has developed what she calls a 'pedagogy of discomfort', a teaching method that actively engages with the uncomfortable emotional dimensions of conversation. She suggests that anger, fear and embarrassment can be psychological defences, which we consciously or unconsciously construct to protect ourselves from learning about certain things. It's a familiar tactic; we've all seen how people derail embarrassing conversations, clapping their hands and saying, 'Anyway!', 'Moving on!' before briskly shifting to a more 'polite subject matter'.

Building on work by Zeus Leonardo, a philosopher at UC Berkeley, Boler focuses on developing methods for 'sitting with' the awkwardness. She suggests that the problem is not discomfort, but inflexibility and a rigid sense of self. We are focused too intently on ourselves and our self-image and fail to recognize that discomfort is in fact a function of a group dynamic, shared by other participants in the conversation.

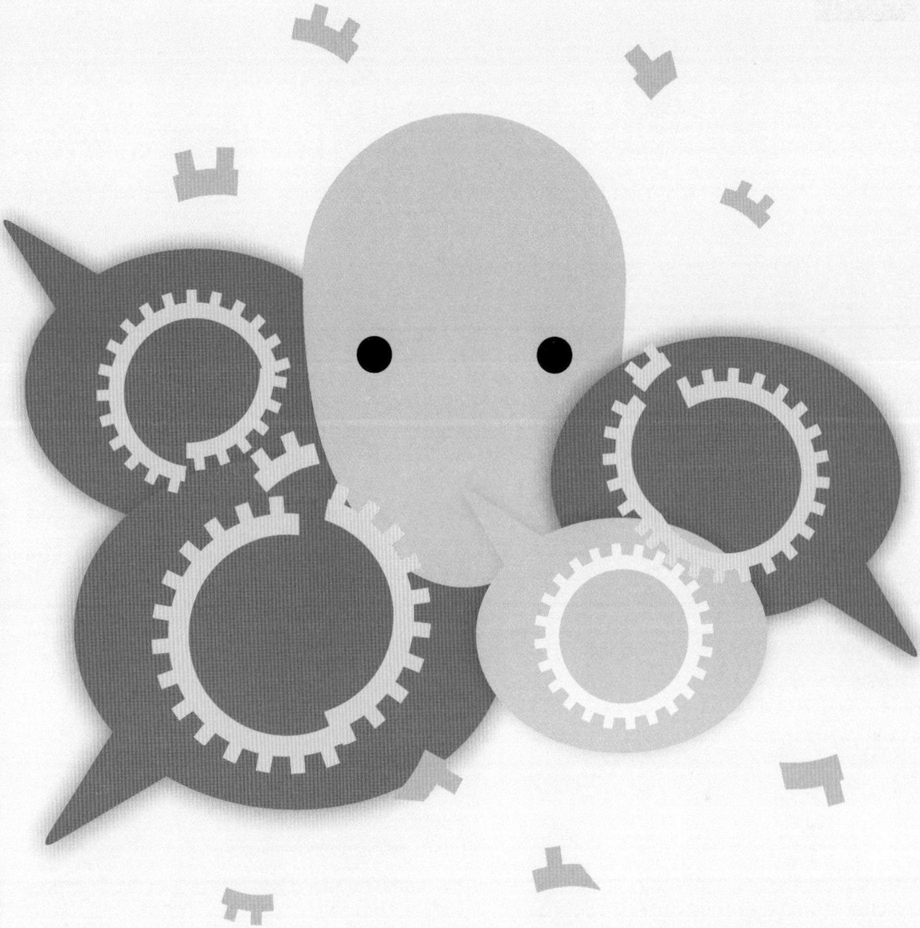

Rather than politely moving a conversation on, we should sit with the discomfort and take it as an indication that we're being challenged in a helpful way. This doesn't mean we can say or do whatever we want – rude, crude or otherwise – when discussing difficult topics. The critique of politeness doesn't mean we should assume 'the gloves are off'. It just makes things more complex.

It encourages us to question how much or how little consideration we should show to our interlocutors. Are they demanding a level of consideration (a politer tone) that is higher than you think they're owed? If the answer is yes, it may be that you can bring this expectation into the open for negotiation. When someone tries to stop a conversation by telling you you're being rude, it may be useful to ask 'why?'.

DISCOMFOR
SIGN WE AR
CLOSE TO S
THAT MATTE

T IS A
E GETTING
UBJECTS
R.

ARGUMENT, DEBATE AND DIALOGUE

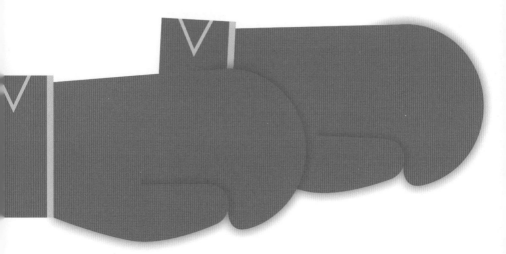

Why do seemingly rational beings go out into the world and argue with each other?

Sometimes it's because we're spoiling for a fight. We've had a bad day and getting into an argument is a way of letting off steam. We might even do it unintentionally. Maybe we've just had some rubbish luck, so we snap at someone as a way of venting.

Perhaps it's because we want people to agree with us. We believe we're right and want others to 'see reason'. Or maybe we just want something – to have pizza for dinner, say – and arguing is a way to get someone to conform to our opinion.

Whatever motivates them, arguments can be painful. They can be exhausting and scary. But they can be exciting, too. Gripping. Thrilling, even. For all the harm they can cause, people actually appear to enjoy or at least be fascinated by them. This fascination isn't a modern phenomenon; since ancient Rome, arguments have been seen as *spectacle*. And with the rise of social media and reality TV, we are now inundated with public confrontation, argument and bickering.

There's often something gladiatorial in the way we argue. In the political and legal sphere, arguments are typically conceived as combative encounters, where separate intelligences vie for supremacy. A 'political debate' consists of two or more positions being put forward, to be 'defended' from attack. This is what the linguist Deborah Tannen calls an 'argument culture' – decisions are reached after a 'trading of blows', a see-sawing between opposing positions – not entirely dissimilar to a pantomime exchange: 'Oh no it isn't!', 'Oh yes it is!', 'Oh no it isn't!'

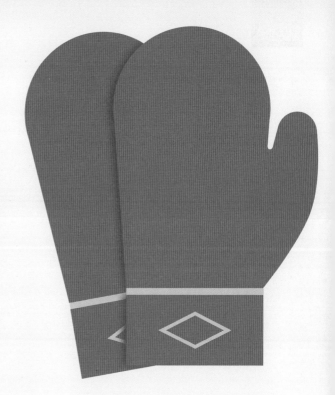

Unfortunately, as a growing number of philosophers are recognizing, these interactions are not particularly productive. If you're invested in defending your original position 'at any cost', it's unlikely you're going to progress in an interesting way. There's no genuine engagement. There's no 'give and take'.

Think, by contrast, how arguments might unfold were participants open to having their minds changed and investigating another person's point of view. Asking questions and shifting positions is more characteristic of 'dialogues' than 'debates'. As the educator Adam Lefstein puts it in his paper 'Dialogic Teaching' (2006): 'Dialogue entails a back-and-forth movement, between my own and the Other's horizons. I am distanced in dialogue from my own prejudices, suspending them in order to engage with the Other.'

Dialogues aren't the kinds of things you can 'win', but when they go well, they produce knowledge and understanding for all parties.

An 'argument', in the colloquial sense, is something you 'get into'. It's a combative exchange. This is the kind of arguing we see in *debates*.

When philosophers talk about arguments, however, they're often thinking of a line of reasoning, which leads via a series of premises towards a conclusion. An argument in this latter sense is something that can be 'built' or 'constructed'. It can be a collaborative act and something that can usefully emerge from a *dialogue*.

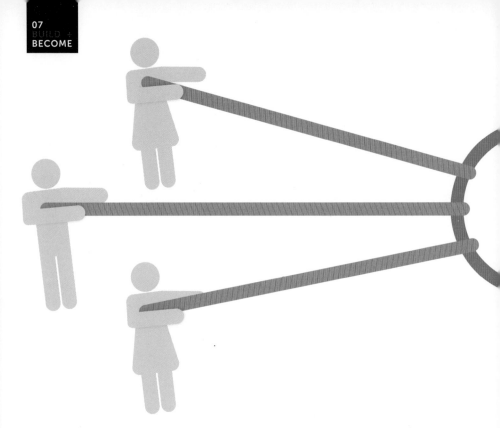

DIALOGUE RATHER THAN DEBATE

When we argue, we're often focused on achieving what the philosopher of education Nicholas Burbules calls 'convergence' (in contrast to 'divergence') of opinion. The aim is to get our partner's thoughts to converge with our own. This leads to what the political theorist Chantal Mouffe calls 'consensus' – a harmonious agreement, where everyone 'consents' to holding a particular view. Debates are typically premised on the idea that discord and dissent are, societally speaking, problems to be overcome through consensus-focused dialogue. In our personal lives and our politics, the thought goes, we should wholeheartedly embrace agreement.

Mouffe, in her book *The Democratic Paradox* (2000), disagrees. She discourages 'consensus politics' and advocates a philosophical outlook that she calls 'agonism', a position that places conflict at the heart of discourse. Unless society is to be dangerously totalitarian (that is, requiring total 'agreement' from its citizens), it needs to be able to negotiate discord and dissent; divergence of opinion is both possible and productive. And in contrast to arguments that are aimed at consensus, dialogues encompass agonistic (if not antagonistic) attitudes.

For Mouffe, however, agonistic dialogue isn't just a matter of politely 'agreeing to

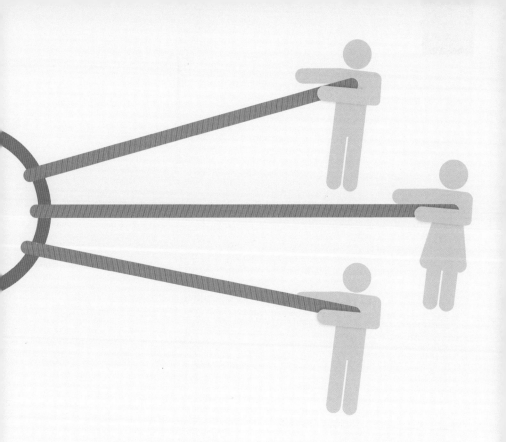

disagree'. It's not about tolerating other people's beliefs and avoiding confrontation. That approach, formalized in the 'reasonable pluralism' of the political philosopher John Rawls, suggests that a 'plurality' of views is fine and dandy just so long as these attitudes are 'reasonable'. For Rawls, 'being reasonable' means not imposing one's own views on other people. For Mouffe, 'being reasonable' is itself an ethical principle emerging out of a particular intellectual context. Like 'being polite', reasonableness is a political attitude – often meaning 'agreeing with the *status quo*'. For Rawls, it's a guiding principle. For Mouffe it should itself be up for discussion.

Think about all the times you've heard someone say, 'Be reasonable', when what they actually mean is 'Be quiet'. Mouffe's view is that these kinds of assertion are far from neutral and shouldn't shape the way we interact with one another.

So where does this leave us? The head-to-head duels, seen in televised debates and work-place arguments, are goal-focused and fascinating to watch, but ultimately they're unproductive. But mechanical nodding and dead-eyed agreement is hardly desirable either. While it sounds painful, 'agonism' is an interesting middle ground between the two, recognizing – and celebrating – how people inevitably rub each other up the wrong way.

IGNORANCE

Every so often we get into arguments without, as they say, 'full possession of the facts'. Maybe, for instance, you criticize your friends for forgetting your birthday without realizing they've organized a surprise party for you. Or perhaps you snap at a colleague for being lacklustre in a board meeting without realizing his boyfriend's just left him.

'I'm sorry,' you say, once he's explained, 'I didn't know!'

Philosophers from Aristotle to Linda Zagzebski have written long and fascinating tracts discussing what it is exactly for us to *know* this, that or the other. Indeed, there's a whole branch of academic philosophy devoted to the topic, known as 'epistemology' – from the Greek *episteme* (knowledge) and *logos* (study of). Philosophers love knowledge. They love having it. They love discussing it too.

Ignorance, by contrast, has received considerably less attention. Traditionally viewed as the inverse of knowledge, it has for a long time been conceived as a kind of absence – a lack – the space where knowledge should be but isn't. In recent years, however, epistemologists have started to re-examine our notions of ignorance, suggesting that this phenomenon is more complex than previously assumed. Moreover, they say, the way ignorance works has consequences for the way in which we engage with one another.

Ignorance comes in different flavours. Consider, for example, the distinction between 'single' and 'double' ignorance that

appears in Plato's dialogues. *Single* ignorance – sometimes called 'Socratic ignorance' – is a matter of knowing that you don't know something. 'All I know,' Socrates famously claimed, 'is that I know nothing!' *Double* ignorance, by contrast, involves not even being aware of what it is that you don't know.

When you hear someone say 'I didn't realize!', they're admitting there's an area of knowledge to which they hadn't had access. When you hear someone say 'That's not *a thing*', they're denying there's an area where there might conceivably be a problem (of which they are ignorant). The former is a case of single ignorance, the latter of double ignorance.

Importantly, people with double ignorance are less likely to be open to other views than those with single ignorance, since they don't even recognize that there are other views. They refuse to acknowledge that there's anything for them to learn. This creates obstacles in arguments. Disagreement is more vexed when your interlocutor fails to acknowledge that there's something you disagree about.

One thing that dialogue can do, when done well, is help reduce double ignorance to single ignorance. This is a form of 'consciousness raising' – increasing awareness of an issue that hasn't yet been recognized by the person you're talking to. Yet the process of reducing double ignorance to single ignorance is often a difficult one, since it typically requires a dramatic shift in someone's worldview.

IT'S JUST COMMON SENSE

In contrast to the traditional idea of ignorance as passive, a number of philosophers have argued that it can be both *active* and *dynamic*. Michele Moody-Adams and Vivian May talk about 'wilful' ignorance. While this is a form of double ignorance, it's not simply an absence of knowledge about knowledge – it's an intentional, *wilful* state, often produced by a particular kind of cultural education.

In her essay 'Trauma in Paradise' (2006), May writes: 'there are many things those in dominant groups are taught not to know, encouraged *not* to see, *and the privileged are rewarded for this state of not-knowing'.*

There are innumerable instances of people actively invested in not knowing something and – consciously or not – making moves to preserve their ignorance. This is not as duplicitous as it sounds. Many of us do it on a day-to-day basis. Imagine someone suggests that your favourite brand of ice-cream is the product of underpaid labour. It's possible you'll want to ignore this information and go about your delicious ice-creaming business. 'I'd rather not know!' you say, as you take another scoop.

Critical race theorists Charles Mills and Linda Martín Alcoff examine a related notion: 'white ignorance'. This is a form of wilful ignorance supported and endorsed by the structures and patterns of a racist, 'white supremacist' society. The philosopher Zara Bain points to the ways in which school systems actively perpetuate certain forms of ignorance to the benefit of white people and the harm of people of colour. Consider, for instance, the way UK history syllabuses prioritize knowledge of Henry VIII over the colonial atrocities performed by the British Empire. Information about Britain's inglorious, racist history is *actively* ignored, while certain kinds of knowledge are systematically given priority.

In a racist society, white people are routinely privileged over people of colour. As beneficiaries of racism, they are also invested in ignoring it. The same is true for cis-gender men in patriarchal societies, and able-bodied people in ableist societies. As Barbara Applebaum notes in her book *Being White, Being Good* (2010), these groups are doubly invested in their ignorance; not only do they benefit from unjust systems, but by ignoring the problem they can tell themselves they're 'morally pure'. Their ignorance isn't neutral – a void, where knowledge should be – it's an actively protected space. As Bain puts it, the ignorance 'resists and fights back'. Consider the way gaps in our knowledge are protected by appeals to 'common sense'. When someone tells you something's 'common sense', they're saying 'Don't investigate!' For a long time it was 'common sense' that the earth was flat, that there was a 'racial hierarchy', and that women didn't have the mental capacity to vote.

These are ignorances that, to extend Bain's metaphor, require *combatting*.

Rather than assuming we know all there is to know about a topic, it can be important to reflect on how knowledge and ignorance inform our deliberation. What is it that we're invested in not knowing? What might someone taking part in our conversation know that we don't?

People sometimes say that 'ignorance is bliss'. Philosophers like Mills, Applebaum, Alcoff and Bain encourage us to ask: bliss for whom, and at what cost?

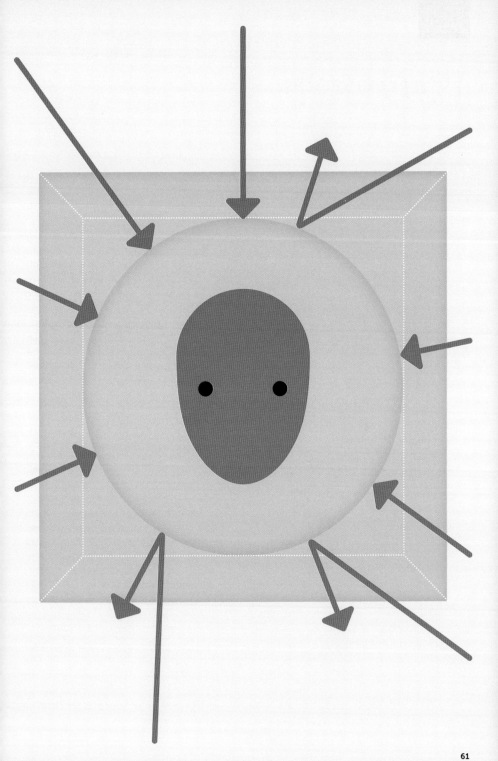

TOOLKIT

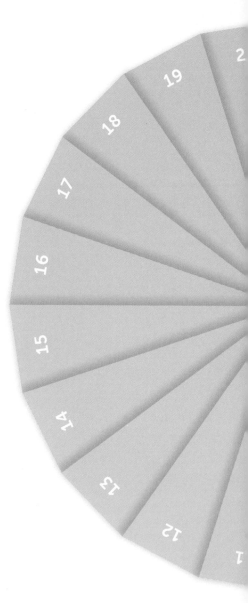

05

We tend to think people should be allowed to 'speak their minds'. However, some philosophers think words can, by themselves, cause harm. Talk to your interlocutor about what is and isn't hurtful and how you might articulate your thoughts without causing harm.

06

We're often encouraged to be 'polite'. But when we try to make conversations run 'smoothly', we sometimes end up withholding uncomfortable but important facts. During 'civil disagreements' it's worth examining whether politeness *helps* or *hinders* conversation.

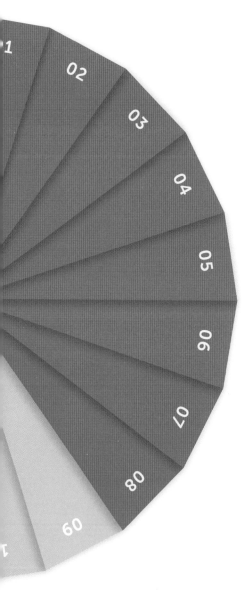

07

Conversations can often end up becoming combative. When engaged in arguments, consider whether you're thinking *against* your interlocutor (seeing them as an opponent) or thinking, dialogically, *with* them.

08

Ignorance is not just the passive absence of knowledge. There are some things we decide we're better off not thinking about – of which we become 'wilfully ignorant'. When confronted with gaps in your knowledge, consider why they might have appeared, and who is benefitting.

FURTHER LEARNING

READ

'The Silenced Dialogue'
Lisa Delpit (*Harvard Educational Review*, 1988)

feministkilljoys.com
Sara Ahmed (2013–)

WATCH

Ash Sarkar DESTROYS . . . herself? In this short YouTube video from Novara Media, the political commentator Ash Sarkar examines the rhetoric and tactics around televised debates.

The Color of Fear. Directed by Lee Mun Wah, this 1994 film is an in-depth look at an intense and emotional confrontation between eight men about race and racism in America.

LISTEN

'Reasonable Men Calming You Down with Moira Weigel', The Dig (Jacobin Radio). In this instalment of the American podcast, Daniel Denvir talks to Moira Weigel about attacks on so-called 'snowflakes'.

VISIT

Café philosophique. Emerging in France in the late 90s, this grassroots organisation operates internationally. Find one – or maybe even found one – in your local area to discuss big ideas over a hot drink and a tasty pastry.

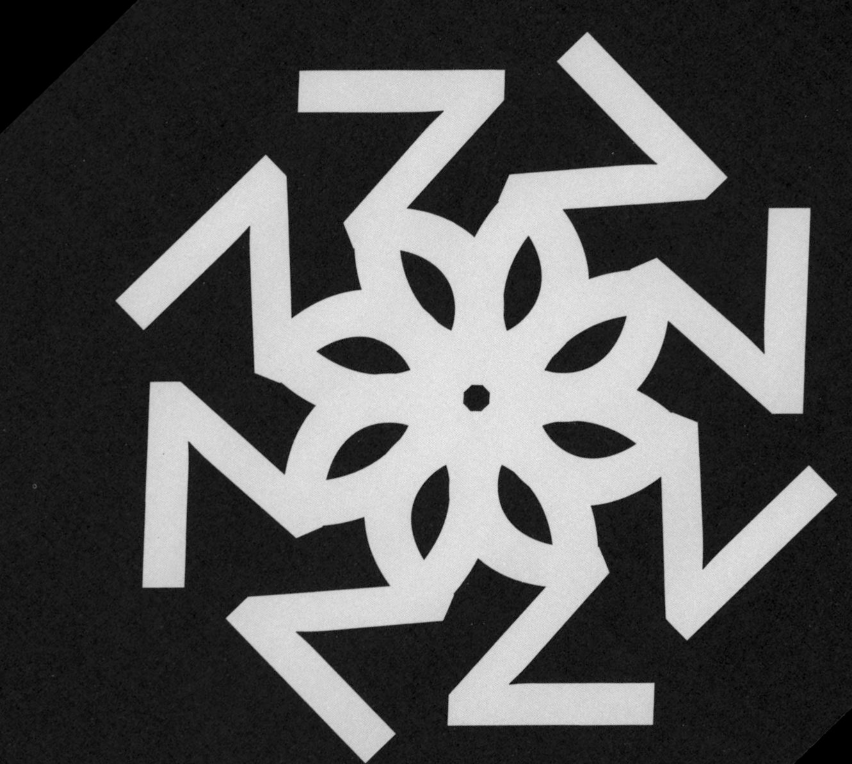

UNDERSTANDING CONFLICT

SECTIONS

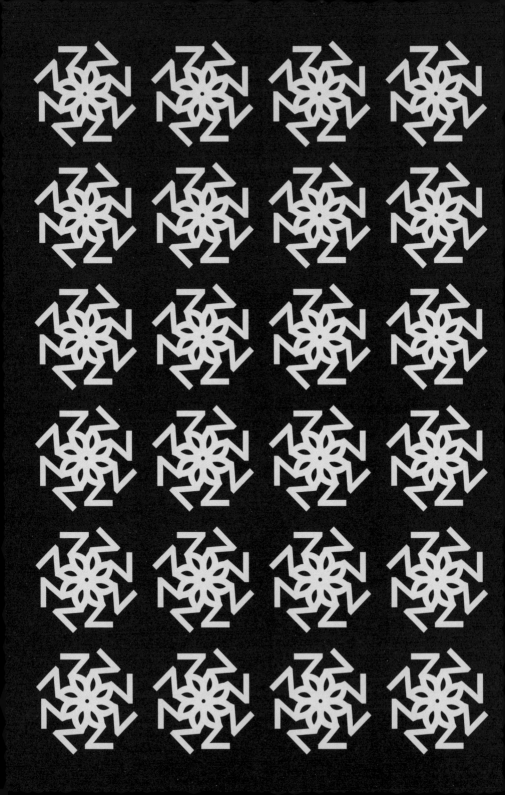

> ' . . . power is not simply what we oppose but also, in a strong sense, what we depend on for our existence . . . '
> Judith Butler

The bad news is: conversation is difficult. Dialogue can run aground even when participants try their best to understand and be understood. You can be clear and kind, considerate and well-meaning, but even then your contributions may end up doing more harm than good. Light-hearted chats can turn into heated arguments, and heated arguments can turn into lifelong feuds.

The good news is: we all know this. At some time or other, we've all been misunderstood or said the wrong thing by accident. And happily, sociologists and philosophers of language have done a fair bit of work identifying and examining the conversational pitfalls we typically slip into. Looking at their research, we can get a better sense of how and why we err. We can learn to identify mistakes and how to avoid them.

Consider, for example, the phenomenon of 'speaking for' others. This is the focus of section 9, 'Talking Over'. All too often, you hear a middle-class white man talking on TV about the experiences of people from marginalized groups. 'Black people experience this', 'The Jewish community experiences that'. Sure, these men may be trying to help, but by talking so loudly – literally and figuratively – are they actually silencing other speakers?

In section 10, 'Going Slowly', we look at two opposite yet equally problematic attitudes to timing. Arguments often revolve around the perceived *urgency*

of a problem: should you 'talk through things slowly'? When is it time 'to stop thinking and start *doing*'? Depending on who you are and the nature of the issue, one or other approach might lead to some unfortunate consequences. Problems may go unaddressed – or be worsened by hurried and ill-considered action.

Section 11, 'Diversions', looks at the way in which power *moves through* speakers in order to shut down conversations that challenge the status quo. Consciously or not, people deploy 'diversionary tactics' in order to shift the focus away from complaints or concerns that destabilize their worldview. It's easily done . . . but not so easily solved. We examine how a 'vigilant' attitude may be useful here.

Lastly, in section 12, 'Panic', we look at the obstructive panic that sometimes sets in when people are forced to confront their own prejudices. Conversations can be shut down as a result of excessive feelings of guilt – or even pessimism about the possibility for progress. Where do you go when it seems that there's nowhere *to* go? How helpful is this spiral of panic?

Of course, these issues may make you feel somewhat nervous even entering a conversation. Don't be disheartened! While common, these kinds of mistakes are relatively easily identified. This chapter is a road map for some of the dead-ends and pot-holes that often pepper conversations.

TALKING OVER

Imagine you overhear the following
exchange between two strangers,
Camila and Peter, in a bar:

P: Hey, what're you drinking?

C: Blauburgunder.

**P: Oh yeah? Looks like a
Pinot Noir to me.**

C: Blauburgunder is a type
of Pinot Noir.

P: Yeah? Are you sure?

C: I'm a sommelier.

P: . . .

C: A sommelier is a specialist
in wine tasting.

Here, Peter is doing what the writer Rebecca Solnit refers to as 'mansplaining' – the act of a man explaining something to a woman, assuming he has the relevant authority and knowledge to speak on a topic, even when the topic in question relates directly to the woman's own experience (these very words – written by male authors – might well constitute an instance of mansplaining). To some it's incredibly awkward. To others it's a form of discursive violence (a violence perpetrated in discourse), where a man implies he has the insight, the authority and the right to talk about whatever he wants, whenever he wants. When a man mansplains, women are positioned as passive audience members, expected to listen even when they know more about the subject than he does.

Now imagine another scenario. Helen and her boyfriend are sitting in a restaurant. Her boyfriend beckons the waiter over.

'I'll have a burger', he says, authoritatively. 'She'll have a Caesar salad, but without the chicken. She hates chicken.'

The waiter takes the order and leaves.

Mansplaining can overlap with the phenomenon known as 'speaking for others'. People speak for others when they step in to articulate what another person, or group of people, is experiencing or what they believe. Helen's boyfriend is speaking for her when he tells the waiter about her taste in food. It can be a similarly violent discursive move; when you speak for someone, you rob them of the opportunity to speak for themselves.

'Speaking for' and 'mansplaining' are forms of what the epistemologist Linda Martín Alcoff calls 'rituals of speaking'. In her essay 'The Problem of Speaking for Others' (1991), Alcoff notes that for us to understand why these speech acts are problematic, we need to understand the whole context – the ritual – of which the words are a part.

Consider, for instance, the following statement: We live in a sexist, patriarchal society where women suffer on a daily basis.

You might be inclined to say that this statement is true in any situation. It's just as true in the mouth of a man addressing a room full of women as it is in the mouth of one of those women. Alcoff, however, notes that the meaning of the sentence is created not just by the words, but by the context in which they're spoken and the social location of the speaker. By explaining this truth about the character of society to a room full of women, a man implies both that his 'audience' is unaware of this fact, and that it's necessary for him to educate them. He is, as a result, reinforcing the very problem he's describing. The same would not be the case were a woman to make the same statement.

Words don't appear out of nowhere. They emerge in specific contexts, spoken by specific people, and the specificity of these things contribute to what those words mean.

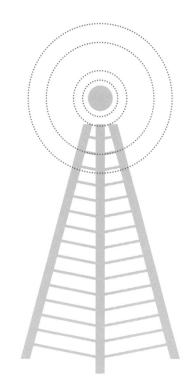

'I'LL BITE MY TONGUE'

Maybe you're worried about speaking for others? Perhaps you think it's better to stay silent except when speaking for, or about, yourself? This is the approach advocated by the feminist philosopher Joyce Trebilcot in her paper 'Dyke Methods' (1988). Trebilcot acknowledges the importance of an open approach to argument – one that resists the drive for consensus – and the first and perhaps most important of the three principles she develops for achieving this is: 'I speak only for myself'.

Given the concerns with 'speaking for', there's clearly some sense to this. However, Alcoff also identifies problems with this move. Trebilcot is proposing what's known as a 'retreat' position. Her approach allows her to absent herself from conversations. Doing so allows people to protect

themselves. It is, as Alcoff identifies, a way of avoiding responsibility and criticism. 'Biting your tongue' doesn't stop you thinking controversial thoughts, it just stops those thoughts from being interrogated.

Alcoff also points out that silence is itself often imbued with meaning. Staying shtum, keeping mum, assuming the role of the bystander, can mean something. Imagine hearing someone say something bigoted in a discussion. Now imagine staying silent. Your silence can be just as much a part of the conversation as the spoken words. Intentional or not, your failure to 'speak out' may well imply that such bigoted comments are permissible.

The issue of 'speaking for' is further complicated by the fact that such speech occurs within an unjust world. As the

philosopher of education Barbara Applebaum suggests, it's often the case that privileged people are better heard than those from marginalized communities. Generally, middle-class white men have greater access to public platforms in the US than do women of colour. White men receive greater 'signal boosting' (their message is broadcast more widely) and are statistically more likely to receive greater credence for what they're saying. Surely, then, it's not only acceptable, but important that the privileged speak for those 'without a voice'? Isn't it *important* to raise awareness, by any means necessary?

Speaking for others is a vexed issue, but one thing that's clear from these analyses is that *context matters*. As such, it's crucial for everyone to be aware of their social location when speaking.

KEEP IN MIND THE FOLLOWING QUESTIONS:
01. **Who are you addressing and why?**
02. **Are you simply talking to fill pregnant pauses?**
03. **Are you talking to hear the sound of your own voice?**
04. **Do you believe you've got a unique perspective on a particular issue?**
05. **Is it more important for you to share these thoughts than to let someone else speak?**
06. **What roles do you take for yourself in the ritual of speaking?**

GOING SLOWLY

'What do we want?'
'Fair pay!'
'When do we want it?'
'NOW!'

The well-known protest cry (where 'fair pay' can be replaced with anything from 'universal suffrage' to 'chocolate') indicates a classic flash-point in uncomfortable conversations: the urgency of change. Determinate action is more pressing for some than others. Fat-cat bosses are less anxious to sort out workers' rights than their underpaid employees. People with health insurance are less worried about supporting national healthcare than those without.

The speed with which you think problems need to be tackled often depends on how interested you are in actually bringing about change. This point is well made by Martin Luther King Jnr in his 'Letter from a Birmingham Jail' (1963). He talks about the softly-softly approach to racial justice employed by 'white moderates':

. . . the Negro's great stumbling block in his stride toward freedom is not the White Citizen Councillor or the Ku Klux Klanner, but the white moderate, who is more devoted to 'order' than to justice . . . who constantly says: 'I agree with you in the goal you seek, but I cannot agree with your methods of direct action'; who paternalistically believes he can set the timetable for another man's freedom . . . and who constantly advises the Negro to wait for a 'more convenient season'. . .

King is critical of the seemingly sympathetic white 'ally' who encourages Black Americans to wait, to *go slowly*. Progress will happen! The dinosaurs will die out! He encourages us to question this assumption; the arc of history *might* bend towards justice, but this doesn't mean we can sit back and hope things will turn out okay. There is no inevitable 'season', nor any asteroid strike to bring an end to the age of racist dinosaurs. The suggestion that there is a natural end towards which humanity is moving allows white moderates to avoid 'direct action'.

King's letter also encourages us to question our devotion to 'order' over 'justice'. You'll often hear people say they 'dislike confrontation', or that they 'try to avoid arguments'. These people privilege politeness over explicitly calling out wrong-doing. As King suggests, this attitude can go hand-in-hand with an implicit commitment to pre-existing structures. The white moderates won't pursue direct action, preferring instead to 'fix the system from the inside'. King is dubious of this approach, as is the scholar-activist and poet Audre Lorde, who famously declared, '. . . the master's tools will never dismantle the master's house. They may allow us to temporarily beat him at his own game, but they will never enable us to bring about genuine change . . .'

Do the 'slow and steady' always win the race? King and Lorde suggest that calls to 'work within the system', to 'bide one's time', can be diversionary tactics that create serious obstacles to social change. There are some situations, as philosopher Sara Ahmed puts it, that demand our 'collective impatience'.

'WHAT ARE WE WAITING FOR?'

Sometimes arguments seem never-ending. Conversation becomes what the essayist Margaret Talbot refers to as an 'academic whirligig' (we theorize round and round and round without any real progress). And yes, this can be frustrating, especially when there's a clear and pressing need for action. Why are we still *talking* about the climate crisis and racism and period poverty? Why haven't we rolled up our sleeves and got stuck in?

This desire 'to get things moving', 'to get the show on the road' is completely understandable – but not entirely unproblematic. All too often impatience can lead to action based on too little information, by well-meaning yet misguided individuals. In her book, *Making Meaning of Whiteness* (1997), Alice McIntyre examines this as an attitude of 'white saviours'. 'White saviours' or 'white knights' are white people who rush to solve problems before fully understanding their various complexities.

It's a paternalistic attitude based on the assumption that the 'saviours' know what's best for those they're trying to save ('paternalism' is derived from the Latin word *pater* meaning 'father' and comes from a time when fathers were widely viewed as heads of the household). It involves muscling into a discussion without having full knowledge of the problems, yet a firm belief that you know how to fix them. Predictably, this attitude often leads to these so-called saviours causing more harm than good.

REFLECTION

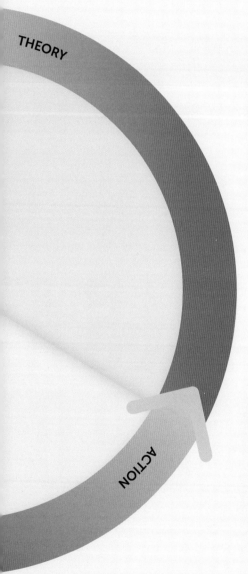

THEORY

ACTION

How do we tread the line between uninformed action and unending chatter? In *Pedagogy of the Oppressed* (1968), the Brazilian educator Paulo Freire recommends 'praxis'. Praxis is an intellectual process in which theorizing informs practice (or action) and vice-versa. It's responsive. You observe a problem and reflect on it, then experiment with actions and refine your practice based on what you've learned. Then you start again.

Think about moving a heavy sofa through a doorway. It's not something you can do by yourself. You can't just ram the sofa through. You've got to size things up, test things out, speak to the person holding the other end of it, gently and carefully move forward.

This kind of approach is best achieved through a 'community of practice', a collaboration in which those who have first-hand experience of the issues (the size and shape of the door, say, or the weight of the sofa) are centrally involved. We see this kind of reflective practice in the American civil rights movement: King's call for direct action was grounded in engagement with the problem and developed in response to the realities of activism.

Praxis, as Freire conceives it, is best achieved through conversation – a particular kind of self-reflective conversation, the collaborative puzzling through of a problem. Whether you're trying to fit a sofa through a doorway, or aiming for gender parity in the workplace, you need to talk to each other. You need to be responsive to lived realities.

SILENCE CA
AS MUCH A
CONVERSA
YOUR SPO

N BE
PART OF
ON AS
EN WORDS.

DIVERSIONS

It's easy to want to escape from uncomfortable conversations. They are, after all, uncomfortable. Whether confronting irascible neighbours about their all-night raves or talking to a parent about their funeral arrangements, we've all been in situations where we've been desperate to 'change the topic'.

Consequently, we've developed various tactics for redirecting the flow of conversations. These tactics involve bolting for the door or feigning coughing fits. There are less obvious ones too. 'Whataboutery' or 'whataboutism' is one of them. Unsurprisingly, it involves asking: 'But what about . . . ?'

It's subtler than some rhetorical moves because it implies that the speaker is engaging with, even recognizing, the importance of what's being said. Doing this allows them to perform a sleight of hand that shifts the conversation onto a less confrontational subject.

Consider the following scenario. It's Friday night and Kathryn is out having drinks with her friends. They're telling her about the extortionate amount they have to pay for rent. Kathryn is from a wealthy family, has never had a job, owns her own home and even has a lodger. One of her friends suggests that Kathryn is 'privileged'. Kathryn replies, defensively, 'Well what about *you*? How many holidays have you taken in the last year? Nine? Ten?'

This is known as the *'tu quoque'* form of whataboutery (from the Latin, 'you too'). It's an attempt to discredit a critic by showing that they are just as guilty as you yourself, and are being hypocritical. Importantly, it doesn't undermine the criticism itself (Kathryn doesn't deny that she's privileged), but rather targets the person making it.

Or imagine that Kathryn's friends are unaware that she owns her own house. She is still profoundly uncomfortable with all this talk of landlords and inheritance, and while nodding sympathetically, she asks, 'What about the rise in homelessness, isn't that dreadful?'

This is another form of whataboutery. The rise in homelessness *is* dreadful – and relevant too – but Kathryn's question derails the conversation. She may not have done it intentionally, but she has effectively redirected a discussion about an issue *in which she is directly implicated* onto something else.

Whataboutery happens all the time. An employer accused of bad business practice may point to other employers whose business practices are even worse. A man may shift the focus from a discussion about misogyny onto one about paternity rights. The scholar and psychoanalyst Deborah Britzman notes that, consciously or not, these moves are deployed in order to avoid engagement with 'difficult knowledge'. The subject under discussion makes the hearer feel uncomfortable, and rather than sit with this discomfort there's an urge to move the conversation along or away. Often the discomfort emerges from the way the topic challenges the hearer's 'moral integrity'. Diversionary tactics allow them to avoid confronting painful but important truths about themselves.

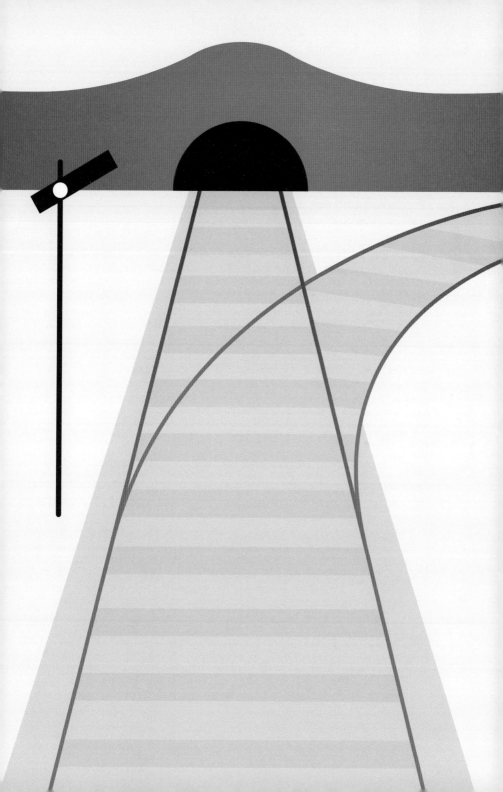

CHECK YOURSELF

Diversionary tactics can distract from a topic entirely, or they can do what scholar-activist Sara Ahmed describes as 'recentring'. That is, they can redirect intellectual labour to centre on the needs of a different group or person. For instance, during a conversation about anti-black racism, a white participant may break into tears (having been accused, perhaps, of complicity in white supremacy). These 'tears' can function to situate the participant as the centre of the discussion. 'Why are they crying?', the group is suddenly led to ask, 'and how can we help them?' This is not a new phenomenon; the intentional deployment of one's tears was known to the Romans as *commiseratio*. In this scenario, the audience is being invited to commiserate with the speaker.

One striking example of commiseratio occurs when powerful men ask others to sympathize with what they construe as powerlessness. The Cornell philosopher Kate Manne points out that this strategy is often deployed to distract attention away from pervasive and pernicious sexism and misogyny. In her book *Down Girl* (2018), she refers to the phenomenon as *'himpathy'*.

The effects of appeals to himpathy are two-fold. When, for instance, men break down in response to accusations of sexual harassment, they claim victimhood. As the American activist and scholar Eve Kosofsky Sedgwick points out, men's tears have a certain social power, especially against the backdrop of traditional notions of masculinity. When men are positioned as stoic, unemotional and strong, their tears are 'more precious' than women's. Consequently, crying when accused of misogynistic behaviour can elicit himpathy and, in fact, position the accused as the victim.

But not only is he positioned as a victim; in the same breath, his own victim – the subject of the misogynistic attack – is positioned as the villain. 'Her accusations will ruin his life' blur into 'She ruined his life, the monster!'

From whataboutery to himpathy, diversionary tactics can be used manipulatively, but they can also be used unconsciously. The best thing to do to guard against diversions and derailment is to stay *vigilant*. If you're being called out or criticized, you might find yourself upset, possibly to the point of tears. You may start crying – and there's nothing wrong with that! You still have a choice, however, whether to use your tears as a reason to no longer engage, whether to continue, or whether to ask if you can 'take a moment'. Consider whether or not you want to continue, stop or pause.

Manne describes the case of the college student, Brock Turner. In 2015, Turner was arrested for sexually assaulting a woman while she was unconscious. A young college athlete, he received an inappropriately lenient sentence after a trial which foregrounded his 'swimming prowess' and the 'severe impact' the conviction would have on his life. The ruling was the result of sympathy, or rather *himpathy*, for Turner over his victim.

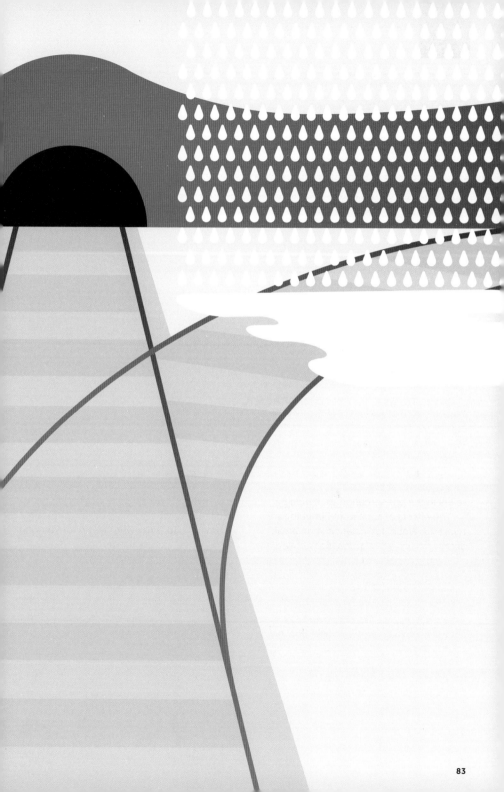

PANIC

Let's face it, we all make mistakes. We misspeak, we can be misunderstood – occasionally we just plain miss the point. And yes, the results can be awkward, or sometimes downright painful.

If you say the wrong thing in the wrong context you risk being called out as foolish or prejudiced or worse. Maybe you told an offensive joke? Perhaps you used a politically incorrect term in the office? Your first reaction might be to deny that you meant it. You were just kidding! You're not *actually* racist!

Often we refuse to even countenance the possibility that we hold bigoted views. Rather than recognizing our own political and moral failings, we become defensive or angry. Sometimes, however, we know we've made an error. The weight of our own bigoted assumptions comes crashing down. We're paralysed by our own failings.

Philosopher of education Ann Diller describes this paralysis as 'torpification', in reference to a peculiar animal called a 'torpedo fish'. This fish makes its philosophical debut in Plato's *Meno*, where the eponymous Meno remarks that through his verbal acrobatics Socrates leaves his interlocutors paralysed like the torpedo fish, which uses an electric ray to zap its victims into a state of numbness. Plato's description is taken up by Diller in 'Facing the Torpedo Fish' (1998), where she applies it to the paralysis that can affect us when we're confronted with our own prejudices. It's

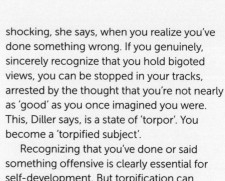

shocking, she says, when you realize you've done something wrong. If you genuinely, sincerely recognize that you hold bigoted views, you can be stopped in your tracks, arrested by the thought that you're not nearly as 'good' as you once imagined you were. This, Diller says, is a state of 'torpor'. You become a 'torpified subject'.

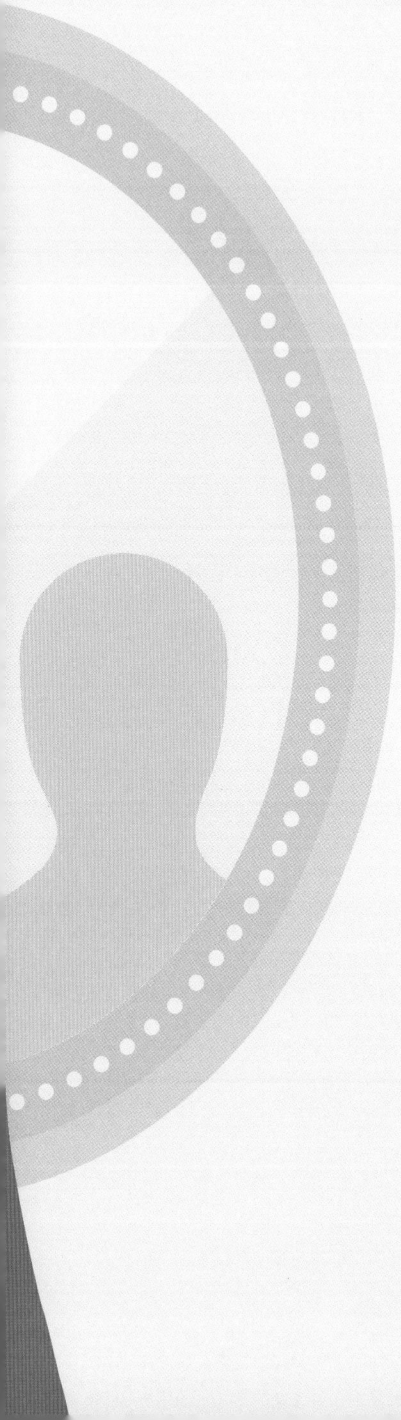

Recognizing that you've done or said something offensive is clearly essential for self-development. But torpification can be pathological too. Consider the hand-wringing young man taking up space at a feminist gathering, explaining how heavily and horribly implicated he is in the problematic structure of our sexist society. He's so mired with guilt and self-hatred that it becomes a form of self-obsession; he sucks energy from the room, demands attention, consumed by his own guilt. 'I'm so privileged,' he says, 'I'm so terrible, and nothing can be done about it.'

As Sara Ahmed points out in *Living a Feminist Life* (2017), statements like this function as confessions; they call for exoneration or forgiveness. Ahmed notes that this is a frequent phenomenon in conversations about race, where white people essentially request that others attend to their feelings of guilt. It's an aspect of what she calls the 'stickiness' of whiteness. In the same moment as confessing their prejudices and privileges, white people are making demands on people of colour.

'WHAT'S THE POINT?'

It's easy to feel a little pessimistic. And pessimism can be further amplified by the thought that, even when we're trying our hardest (perhaps *especially* when we're trying our hardest), we may end up contributing to the problem. So what's the point? What's the point in political action? In ethical behaviour? Why should we bother when none of it amounts to a hill of beans?

These questions are the focus of Derrick Bell's *Faces at the Bottom of the Well* (1992), where the law professor advances a position that he calls 'Racial Realism'. Racial Realism is a response to optimistic declarations about political progress and claims about overcoming racism in America.

Black people will never gain full equality in this country. Even those Herculean efforts we hail as successful will produce no more than temporary 'peaks of progress', short-lived victories that slide into irrelevance as racial patterns adapt in ways that maintain white dominance.

Claims about progress and 'solutions to racism' are, for Bell, always delusions. We need to be realistic, he says. We aren't going to be saved by deliberative democracy or automatic progress. Suggestions to the contrary are unhelpful. The philosopher Calvin L. Warren has developed this view in his book *Ontological Terror* (2019), writing that 'humanist *affect* (the good feeling we get from hopeful solutions) will not translate into freedom, justice, recognition or resolution . . .' In both Bell and Warren's work, we see a clear articulation of the downsides to optimistic humanism. It feels nice to be hopeful, but this 'affect' is a distraction.

It's unsurprising, perhaps, that Bell's publishers worried his work would be too despairing for mainstream audiences. To this, Bell is said to have responded: 'You don't understand. For a black person in this society, the truth is never despairing.' In contrast to the torpified subject described by Diller, Bell says the appropriate response to a pessimistic worldview is not inaction, but continued action. Things may appear hopeless, but we should struggle on regardless – we should continue the conversation. This view is also found in the work of the philosopher George Yancy, who recognizes the futility of trying to overcome certain deeply ingrained prejudices, but also acknowledges the importance of the attempt. For Yancy, men can be 'anti-sexist sexists', and white people can be 'anti-racist racists'. We might never be able to overcome prejudices but that shouldn't stop us from trying.

Bell, who died in 2011, put his theory into practice. Indeed, it was as a result of his attempts to diversify the university faculty that he lost his professorship at Harvard Law School. In 1990, his requests for the tenured appointment of a black female professor were dismissed, but he carried on anyway, until his own tenure was terminated. In 1998, the school's first black female tenured professor, Lani Guinier, was appointed – which Bell would certainly have seen as a cause for celebration . . . but probably not hope.

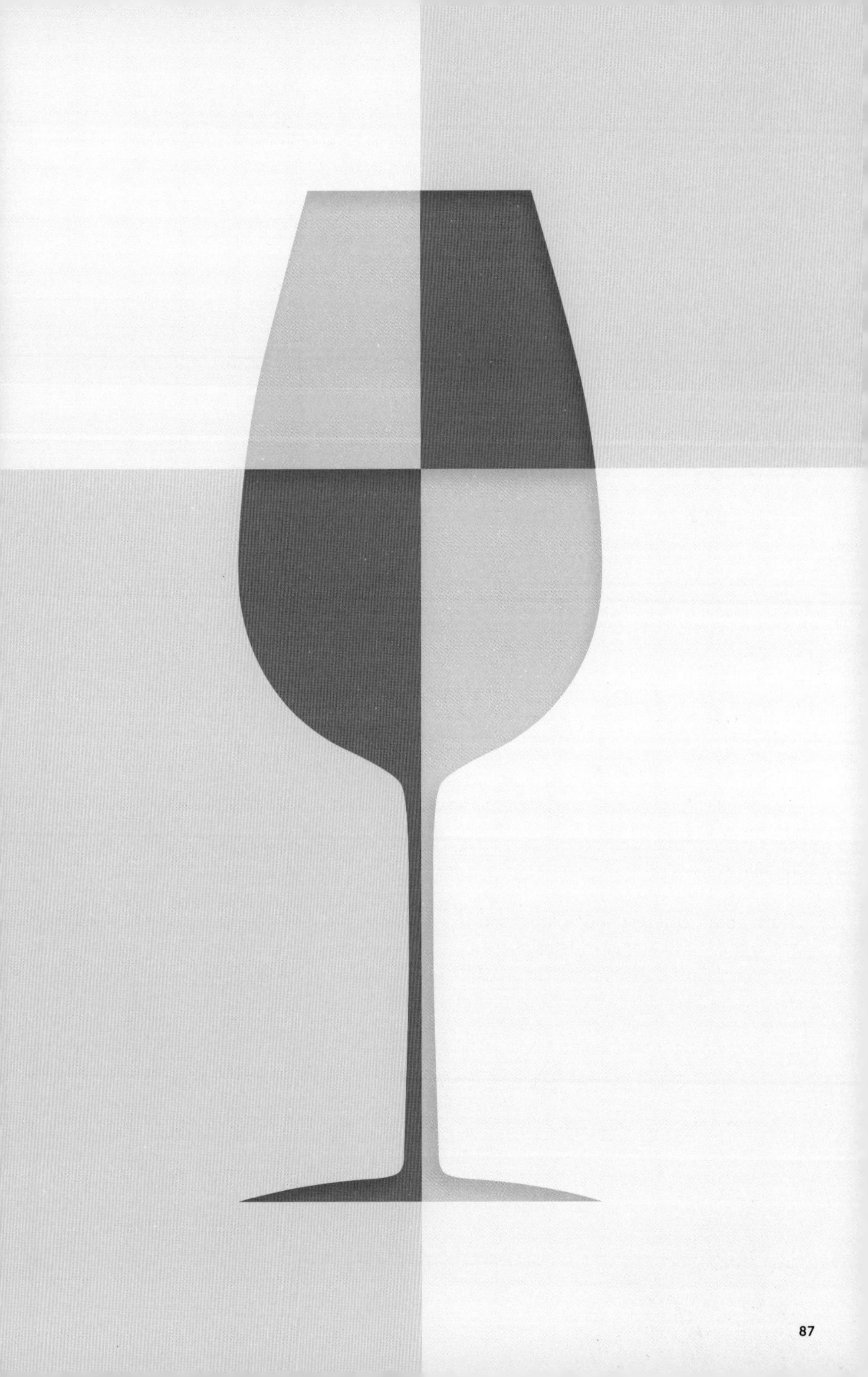

TOOLKIT

09

The meaning of a statement or an argument depends on the words used, but also on the context in which they're spoken and the person saying them. Think about how you are being read, and how you are reading others.

10

Sometimes, when advocating change, we're told to 'go slowly', to 'take our time'. This is often said by people who aren't personally invested in bringing about change. When considering the urgency of an issue, discuss who does and doesn't have 'skin in the game'.

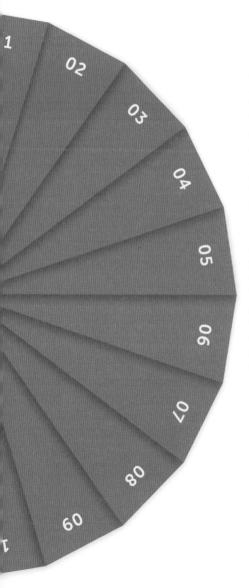

11

Typically, we want to avoid awkward conversations. Yet discomfort, awkwardness, anger and defensiveness are important parts of disagreements. Pay attention to the emotions that arise during the conversation. What sense do you have of how your interlocutor feels?

12

When confronted with something that challenges you, it's easy to panic and want to run away, literally or figuratively. It's worth examining *why* you feel so uncomfortable – are you scared you might be prejudiced? Try to sit with this and consider how to address it.

FURTHER LEARNING

READ

Down Girl: The Logic of Misogyny
Kate Manne (Oxford University Press, 2018)

WATCH

Produced as part of an HBO anthology movie, 'The Space Traders' (*Cosmic Slop*) is based on a short science fiction story written by the lawyer and anti-racist activist Derrick Bell.

'Context' (*Stewart Lee's Comedy Vehicle*, Series 3, Episode 4). In this episode of his BBC show, the comedian Stewart Lee examines the concept of 'offence' and searches for a 'context-free word'.

LISTEN

Building on her work in *Why I'm No Longer Talking To White People About Race*, Reni Eddo-Lodge's podcast conducts a deep-dive into discussions around racism and anti-racism: aboutracepodcast.com

VISIT

Bristol Festival of Ideas. Established in 2005, the Bristol-based festival aims to bring people together to discuss pressing issues, from the climate emergency to white supremacy and women's rights.

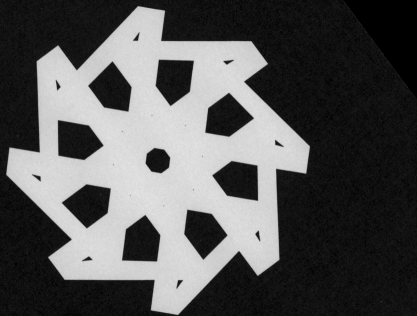

REACHING OUT

SECTIONS

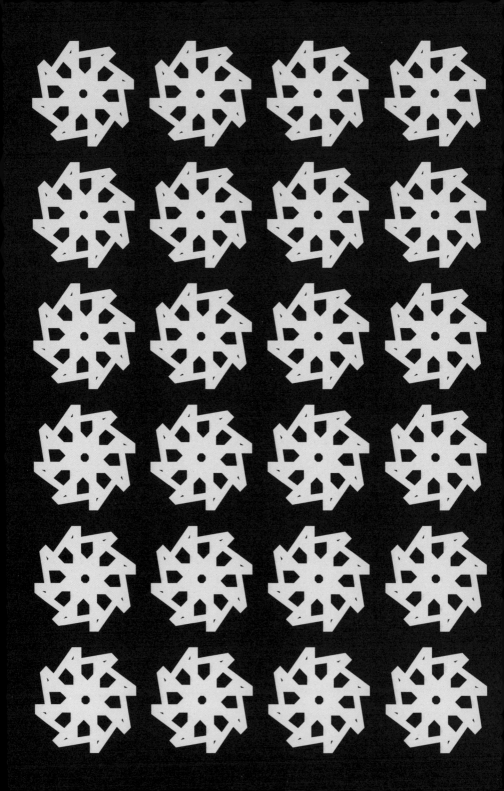

'If you have come here to help me, you are wasting your time. But if you have come because your liberation is bound up with mine, then let us work together.'
Lilla Watson

Every so often we meet people who just 'get us'. They're 'on the same page', 'the same wavelength', we just 'vibe'. And that's great – it's *fantastic*, really – partly because it's so incredibly unlikely. Think about all the tiny historical details and psychological nuances that contribute to you feeling and thinking and living in the wonderfully peculiar way that you do. It's surprising, then, given the bountiful diversity of human experience, that any two people can meet and find themselves thinking even roughly the same things.

Of course, not everyone enjoys an immediate connection. We don't all see eye to eye. And thank goodness! Can you imagine how boring it would be if there was no diversity of opinion? This fact, however, leaves us with a puzzle. How do we *get* on the same wavelength as other people? What can we do to nurture productive dialogue? The aim of this chapter is to try and answer these questions.

In section 13, 'Solidarity', we consider two types of relationship that can hold between members of different political groups. On the one hand, people can declare themselves 'allies'. On the other, they can declare 'solidarity'. What do these related relationships entail? Is there something patronizing about the notion of allegiance?

Sometimes the best way to nurture connections is with a nice cup of tea and a biscuit. Section 14, 'Meal-sharing', examines the idea of 'inter-dining' and outlines the ways that communal eating can nourish mutual understanding. Meals don't typically tend to be goal-oriented (the aim of a dinner isn't to reach the dessert); as such they also serve as a good model for open dialogue.

Humour is the focus of section 15 – and jokes, it turns out, can be a surprisingly serious business. It's clear there's considerable potential for humour to create boundaries and exclude people from conversations (some individuals just don't 'get it'). At the same time, jokes can bring people together and create feelings of kinship and shared sentiment.

In section 16 we're going to look at 'Education'. The work of heavy thinking isn't always evenly distributed (some speakers are required to do more explanatory work than others), and awareness of this is crucial for genuinely generative discussions. Here, we're going to explore the importance of self-education. One helpful way to get on the same page as someone else is to read the same book.

Sometimes you meet someone and everything you say seems inappropriate. All your jokes fall flat. You come across as rude, insensitive or ignorant (or all of the above). In this chapter we'll look at why this happens and what we can do to make understanding easier.

SOLIDARITY

Every year on 8 March, people around the world celebrate International Women's Day. And every so often a well-meaning male celebrity 'lends their voice' to the cause and speaks up for women's rights on large audience platforms like TV or social media. 'It gives me a lot of hope,' said one such celebrity, 'to see so many women leaders finally taking their place, their rightful place, in the power structure.' Such declarations are taken to be signs of 'allyship' or 'allegiance'. (The same could be said of two men starting a section in their philosophy book with such comments about International Women's Day.)

In social justice terms, an ally is a member of a group with a level or type of privilege who 'stands up for' and 'lends their voice to' oppressed groups who don't have that privilege. A man championing women's rights is one example. A white person speaking out against racism is another, as is a straight person defending gay marriage, or a member of the wealthy elite speaking for the 99 per cent.

Being an ally appears, at first, to be a good thing. Allies are well intentioned and want to help out. Their heart's in the right place. They recognize their privileges and want to use them for good. It's no surprise that in this example the male celebrity was celebrated as a 'good guy' for what he said, and for his continued commitment to gender equality.

At the same time, there's something slightly iffy about allies. It seems a little strange that so much attention is paid to what *men* have said on International Women's Day.

This is an example of what Sara Ahmed calls 'the stickiness' of privilege. In trying to stand up for women, the male celebrity garners positive attention as a *man*.

The relationship between the ally and the oppressed group is problematically asymmetric – it goes one way. The power imbalance that International Women's Day is intended to address can in fact be exacerbated by the 'charitable' attitude of men. The legitimacy that male allies trade on when 'speaking for' women can be reinforced rather than reduced by these statements of allegiance (we talk more about this in section 9, 'Talking Over'). Irrespective of their intentions, these supposedly helpful voices are picked up and broadcast in a way that drowns out the voices of women.

In her piece 'On Making Black Lives Matter' (2016), the American essayist and activist Roxane Gay examines this problem in relation to 'white allies'.

Black people do not need allies. We need people to stand up and take on the problems borne of oppression as their own, without remove or distance. We need people to do this even if they cannot fully understand what it's like to be oppressed for their race or ethnicity, gender, sexuality, ability, class, religion, or other markers of identity. We need people to use common sense to figure out how to participate in social justice.

Here, Gay problematizes the concept of an ally – but points to a related notion that may, perhaps, be more useful: Solidarity.

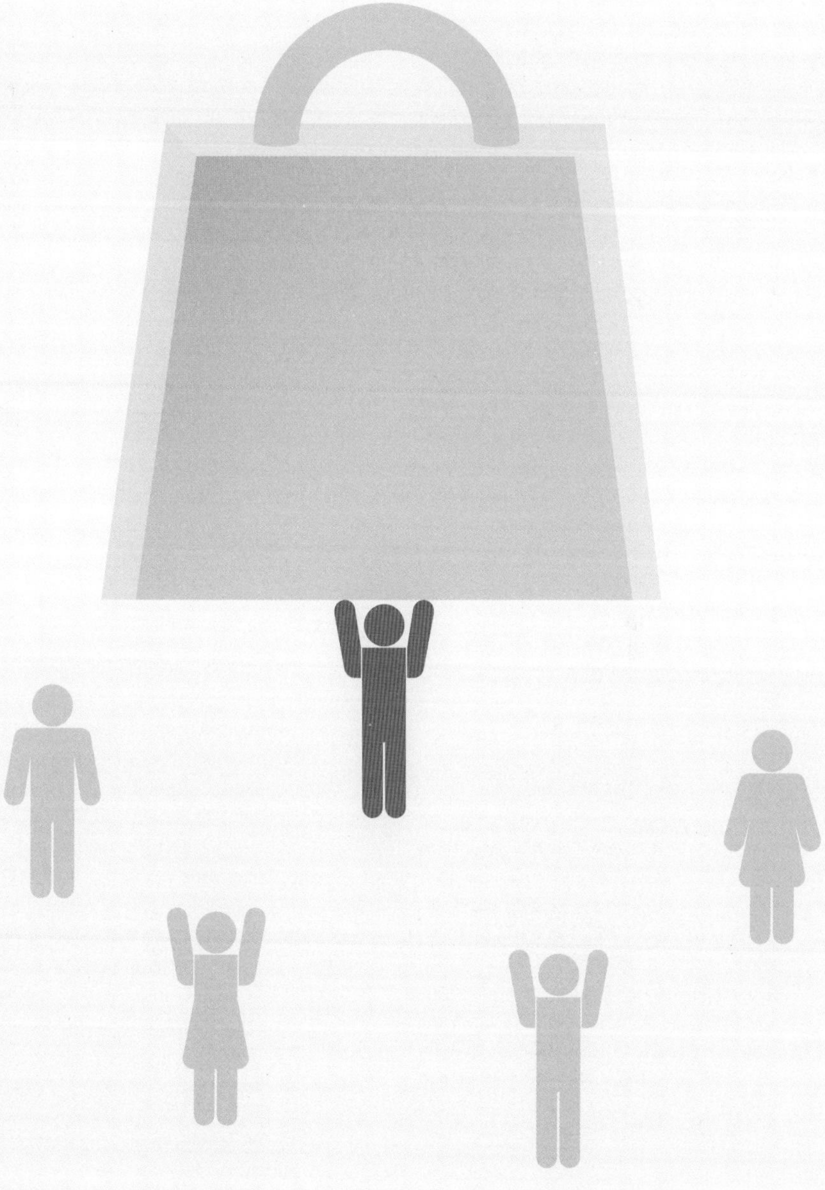

SHARE THE LOAD

In the mid-1980s over 150,000 miners went on strike across the UK to protest against widespread pit closures by Margaret Thatcher's Conservative government. These strikes lasted for over a year and Britain's mining towns and communities suffered terribly. Throughout the industrial action, the miners received support from what was seen, at the time, to be an unlikely quarter: 'Lesbians and Gays Support the Miners' was a group of lesbians and gay men based primarily in London, formed to fund-raise for the striking miners. The LGSM declared their solidarity with the miners and raised considerable funds to help their cause, as well as appearing with them on picket-lines and at protests.

Solidarity is a common theme in philosophical and political works, from Aristotle onwards. It's a specific kind of relationship that can hold between individuals and groups. As Waheed Hussain describes it in 'The Common Good' (2018), solidarity requires the elevation of another's interests to the same status as one's own. The members of the LGSM saw the governmental attacks on the miners as attacks upon themselves – the miners' interests and concerns were treated as though they were concerns for the LGBTQ+ community (as dramatized in the 2014 film, *Pride*). Here, we see the realization of Roxane Gay's demand for people 'to stand up and take on the problems borne of oppression as their own'.

Importantly, declarations of solidarity do not require consensus. People don't need to agree in order to act in solidarity. Solidarity typically crystallizes around particular issues, but agents need not agree on all issues. As Naomi Scheman puts it in her paper 'Queering the Center by Centering the Queer' (1997): 'The issue . . . is not who is or is not really whatever, but who can be counted on when they come for any one of us: the solid ground is not identity but loyalty and solidarity.'

Allyship is an asymmetric relationship. It works one way; someone enters a debate and 'helps out' someone else. That's why, in the face of systemic anti-black racism, it doesn't make much sense to talk of 'black allies to white people'. Unlike allyship, however, solidarity can be a reciprocal relationship. In 1984, the LGSM group declared its solidarity with the striking miners. Shortly afterwards, the miners marched with the LGBTQ+ community at Gay Pride and voted as a block to advance LGBTQ+ rights.

Solidarity is a powerful political force. It isn't a matter of 'lending your voice' or temporarily mobilizing your privilege. It's a matter of recognizing the ways injustices intersect, and how the fates of marginalized groups are bound together. It's a matter of acknowledging that misogyny adversely affects men as well as women, that heterosexism damages straight people as much as gay people, that racism harms everyone, that capitalism isn't just a problem for the poor. The word 'solidarity' comes from the Latin 'solidum', meaning 'whole'. When you declare solidarity you position yourself as a part of a whole – and you're all the stronger for doing so.

MEAL-SHARING

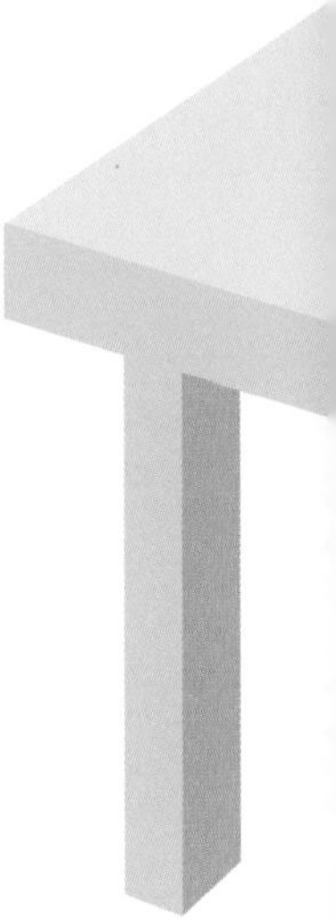

We argue over email and WhatsApp and Twitter. We argue on our mobiles and Reddit and Facebook. Technology has advanced to such an extent that we can sit in our bedrooms in Atlanta and pick fights with people sitting in their living rooms in Kuala Lumpur. We can argue without even knowing who we're talking to.

Social media technologies have brought people together. They have great liberatory potential, linking up different folk around the globe. But they can exacerbate disagreements too. It's harder to gauge emotional reactions, to see your respondent as a person, if they've been reduced to a few dancing pixels. It's easier to caricature them, to flatten them into a stereotype, if you only have a shallow understanding of who they are and where they're coming from.

This problem is hardly new. Communities that are geographically or socially separate inevitably tend to understand each other less well than those that exist in proximity.

The thought, advanced by the scholar-activist Nathaniel Adam Tobias ~~Coleman~~, is that in order to puzzle through disagreements it's important to be aware of these distances. People with different views and from different walks of life can profit from brushing up against each other. One of the best ways to do this, suggests ~~Coleman~~, is through meal-sharing.

Meal-sharing means exactly what it says on the tin: sharing meals. In 'The Duty to Miscegenate' (2013), ~~Coleman~~ examines meal-sharing, or 'inter-dining', as a method for tackling inter-cultural tensions. This work builds on that of Bhimrao Ambedkar, the Indian economist and social reformer who was heavily involved in campaigns against social discrimination of the Dalit caste (the 'untouchables') in India in the early twentieth century. In 'The Annihilation of Caste' (1936), he advocates regular inter-caste dinners as a means of fostering fellowship. Members of distinct castes can better understand one another when engaged in that most human of practices: getting a bite to eat.

For ~~Coleman~~, the importance of inter-dining can be explained partly in relation to the symbolic power of meals; to offer someone 'a place at the table' is a way of expressing fellowship. It's no accident, ~~Coleman~~ says, that 'companionship' is etymologically grounded in the Latin words '*con*' (with) and '*panis*' (bread). A companion is someone with whom we 'break bread'.

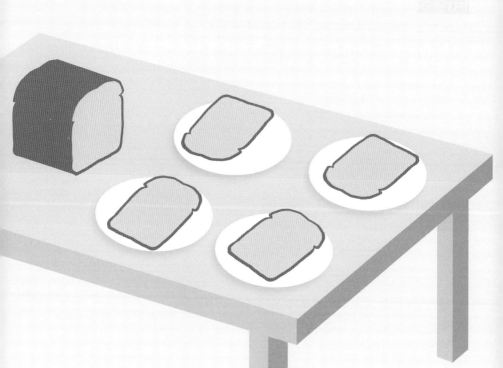

The effectiveness of meal-sharing in nurturing dialogue is borne out by the science. ~~Coleman~~ describes various sociological studies conducted in South Africa in the early 2000s, which show that racial reconciliation between black and white South Africans was non-accidentally related to 'inter-group contact at meal-times'. This correlates to what the psychologist Gordon Allport calls 'the contact hypothesis': certain forms of inter-group contact reduce the prejudices holding between them. It's not hard to see how meal-sharing can do this. We associate eating together with intimacy. Intimacy creates companionship. Companionship is good in itself, but also provides foundations for agreement and decision-making – and that, as they say, is the icing on the cake.

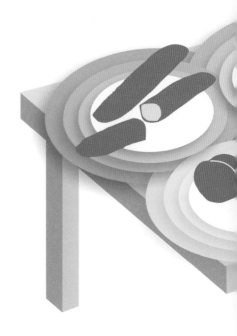

'LET'S EAT!'

Meals can bring us closer together. Office tensions can be dissolved over a plate of chips in the pub. Family discord may be soothed with an outing to the local carvery. Still, it's not inevitable that meals are relaxing. We've probably all eaten in restaurants or at people's houses where we've felt out of place. Maybe you have specific dietary preferences that aren't being met? Maybe you're confused about which piece of cutlery to use? Sometimes this discomfort is something to be avoided (we discuss this further in section 17, 'New Spaces'), but it might not always be such a bad thing.

Going round to someone's house for a meal can be an example of what the feminist philosopher and activist Maria Lugones calls 'world-travelling'. Putting yourself 'out

there', in someone else's dining room or favourite restaurant, helps you understand 'where they're coming from'. Sure, it might be nerve-wracking – you might accidentally insult them or end up eating food you're not used to – but you may also gain important insights into their world, where they're comfortable and in control. Your anxiety can be a good sign, showing that you're moving out of your own comfort zone and into theirs.

Lugones is emphatic in saying that world-travelling isn't just a matter of tasting new, 'exotic' flavours, or indeed even literally travelling. When world-travelling, there should be genuine attempts to engage with the *whole* world, not just the culinary aspects. As the novelist Jamaica Kincaid

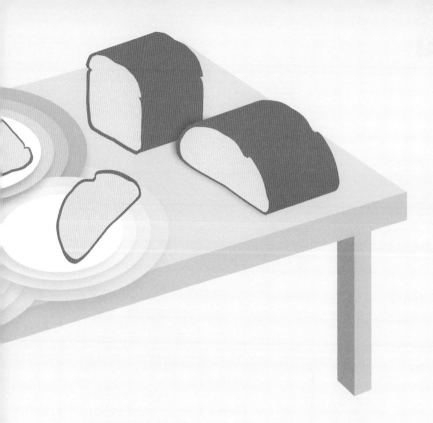

puts it, it's important to avoid becoming mere tourists, 'pausing here and there to gaze at this and taste that'. World-travelling is about opening yourself up and appreciating all the linguistic and societal conventions that surround the meal. Of course, these conventions may make you feel uncomfortable (Are you eating this correctly? Have you mispronounced the name of the dish?), but this discomfort is the product of a disparity in world-views, your own and your host's. The longer you sit with it the more likely you are to understand where your co-diner is coming from.

Importantly, world-travelling and meal-sharing are not goal-oriented. It's the sharing of the meal that's important, not the replenishing of energy. It's about the journey not the destination. In this respect, meals serve as an excellent model for open conversation. People come together, not with an end-goal in mind, but with the hope of being in each other's company. While arguments are often thought of as linear processes – directed towards reaching a Decision, a Solution or General Consensus – they can also be seen as opportunities to interact with and get to know other people. As Kwame Anthony Appiah puts it in *Cosmopolitanism* (2006): 'Conversation doesn't have to lead to consensus about anything, especially not values; it's enough that it helps people get used to one another.'

A good conversation, like a good meal, isn't something you aim to finish. It's something you hope to enjoy.

SOLIDARITY
A POWERF
POLITICAL

IS

FORCE.

HUMOUR

'I was only joking!'

That's what people say when they're trying to back-pedal. Maybe they've insulted your new haircut. Maybe they've made fun of your project pitch in a meeting. Maybe you tell them it hurt your feelings, it upset you, it made you uncomfortable, and maybe they shrug and say, 'I didn't *mean* it.' Or 'Don't be so sensitive.' Dismissing a statement as a 'joke' is often a defensive strategy, where the speaker attempts to distance themselves from the offence they've caused. 'I wasn't being serious.'

Eva Dadlez and Aaron Smuts think there's no such thing as 'only' joking. Jokes, as they punctuate our everyday life, are more than mere verbal flourishes; they're important linguistic events, often demonstrating a complex mastery of language and meaning-making. They can play central roles in group dynamics and the conversations of which they're a part. Dadlez and Smuts' research is part of a growing body of philosophical literature that encourages us to take joking, and humour in general, more seriously: jokes, they say, mean something.

One area that has recently risen to prominence in this literature is the ethics of jokes. To some, the phrase itself may sound like a punch-line or a category error. Jokes are just jokes, they're not subject to ethical critique, they're not the kind of thing that can be right or wrong or good or bad. Such deflationary thoughts lie behind defences of what many think of as 'politically incorrect' humour. They're just words, the deflationist says, and as the old adage goes, 'Sticks and stones may break my bones, but words will never hurt me.' When someone says 'Can't you take a joke?', the implication is that ethical or moral critique of a humorous statement is inappropriate, because utterances by themselves are harmless.

Of course, anyone who's ever been laughed at or made fun of will see the weakness of the 'just a joke' position. Humour can be harmful. It *can* create boundaries and function to exclude specific listeners. Some people are positioned as 'in on the joke' and others are not. Some people 'get it' and other people don't.

Philosophers of language like Nadia Mehdi analyse jokes as 'speech acts'. A speech act is a verbal utterance (someone saying something out loud) that both conveys information *and* performs an action. The classic example of such an act is the declaration 'I do' in a marriage ceremony. 'I do' both expresses the speakers' agreement *and* it consummates the marriage. Jokes, Mehdi thinks, do things too. For instance, they can undermine the legitimacy of certain perspectives. Sexist jokes about 'women drivers' reinforce the sexist idea that women are less capable of driving than men. Jokes about 'global Jewish conspiracies' perpetuate anti-Semitism, and in turn cause listeners to ignore or fail to hear Jewish concerns about institutional anti-Semitism.

A joke need not be explicitly offensive for it to create boundaries. Think about the 'office clown' (there's always one). When they joke around, some of the office personnel are 'in on the joke', but who's outside it? Is the office clown making fun of someone? Does that someone feel excluded as a result?

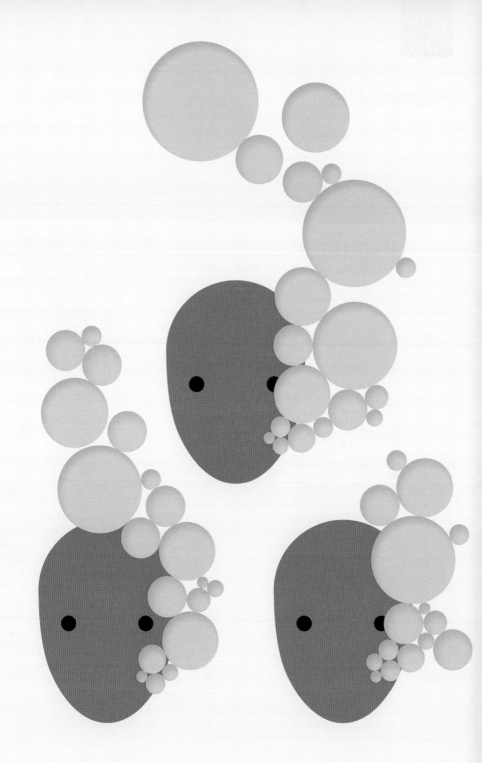

'GET IT?'

*It is already noteworthy that we laugh at all,
at anything, and that we laugh all alone. That
we do it together is the satisfaction of a deep
human longing, the realization of a desperate
hope. It is the hope that we are enough like
one another to sense one another, to be able
to live together.*

Jokes can exclude people. That's the
downside. They can create walls. The upside,
as Ted Cohen describes above in *Jokes:
Philosophical Thoughts on Joking Matters*
(1999), is that not all walls are bad. Some
provide shelter. Some boundaries bring
people closer together.

Imagine walking into a meeting with a
group of people you've never met. Before
getting down to business, you engage in
small-talk.

'How was your trip?' someone asks. 'Did
you take the train?'

You mention you flew in from Edinburgh —
and add, 'Boy, are my arms tired!'

It's an old joke (a very old joke), and you
make it *because* you're nervous. Still, the
others laugh. They're laughing because
they know it's an old joke — and they're fully
aware of what a 'dad joke' is (the kind of joke
that makes you groan rather than chuckle).
Everyone's 'gets it'. In this situation, Cohen
says, the joke serves as a conversational
shorthand; it points to shared understanding
that would otherwise take considerable time

and effort to express. A group boundary is
drawn and everyone present falls within it.

Imagine, by contrast, what happens if the
joke 'falls flat'. Perhaps it's met with bemused
scowls. '*Why* are your arms tired?' Cohen
think the sense of dislocation that results
when a joke 'fails to land' is highly telling. It's
a failure of communication, the result of a
lack of shared cultural touchstones, and as
such you feel excluded. Not only do people
not 'get it', they don't 'get you'.

Jokes can include or exclude listeners.
They can bring people in and strengthen
bonds of friendship, or they can keep people
out and undermine their legitimacy. More
often than not, these speech acts work
differently depending on the context in which
they're uttered. A joke which involves an
intimate understanding of your family history
and your relationship with your mother,
brother and second-cousin-twice-removed
may leave your siblings in stitches and bring
you closer together. If you're talking to your
siblings in front of your partners, however,
cracking the same joke may create an 'us/
them' dynamic. Insiders and outsiders.

The practice of joke-telling is a funny old
business. Whether they make you laugh or
not, jokes *do* things. Humour can marginalize
and silence people — or it can nurture
intimacy and a positive group identity.
Whatever they are, it seems that jokes are
never *just* jokes.

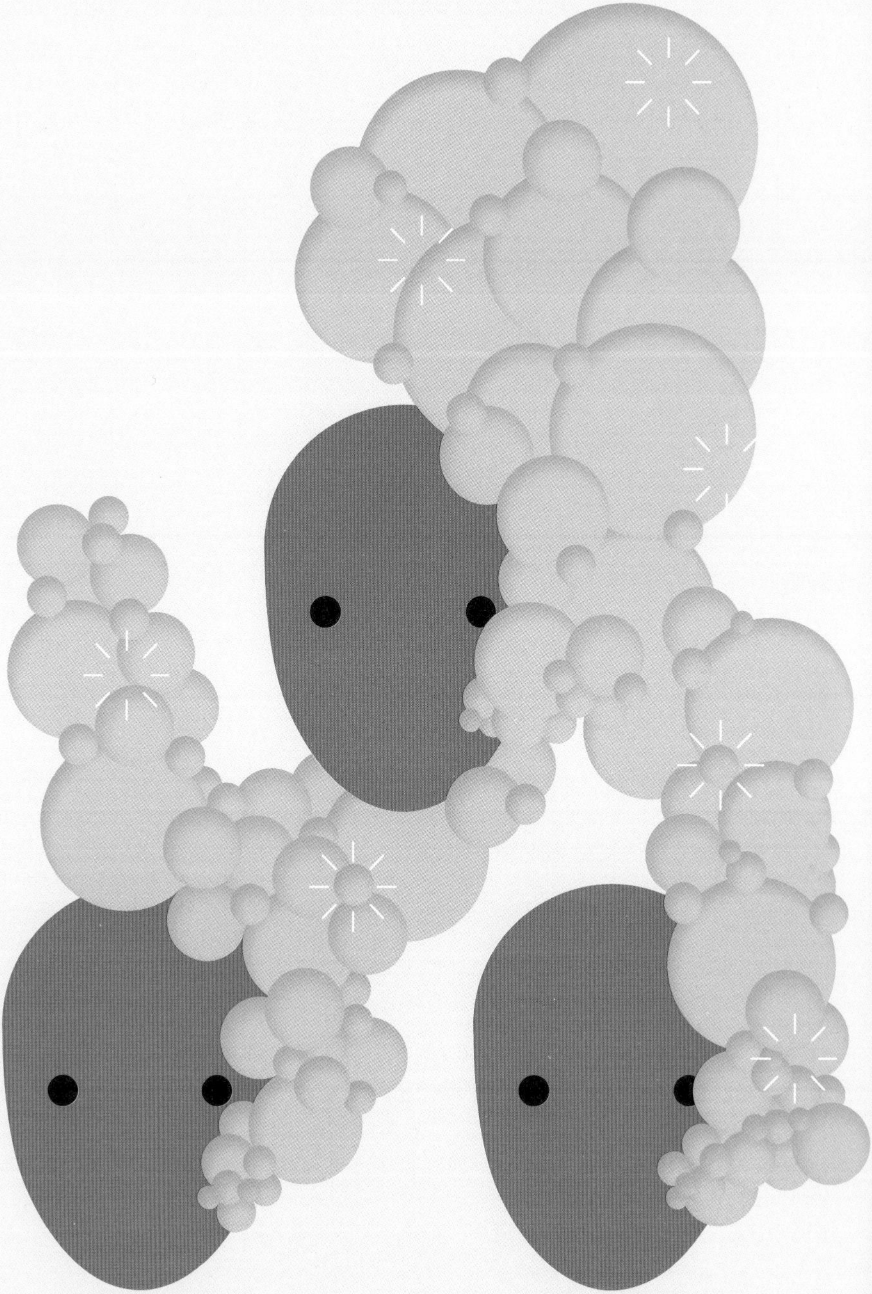

EDUCATION

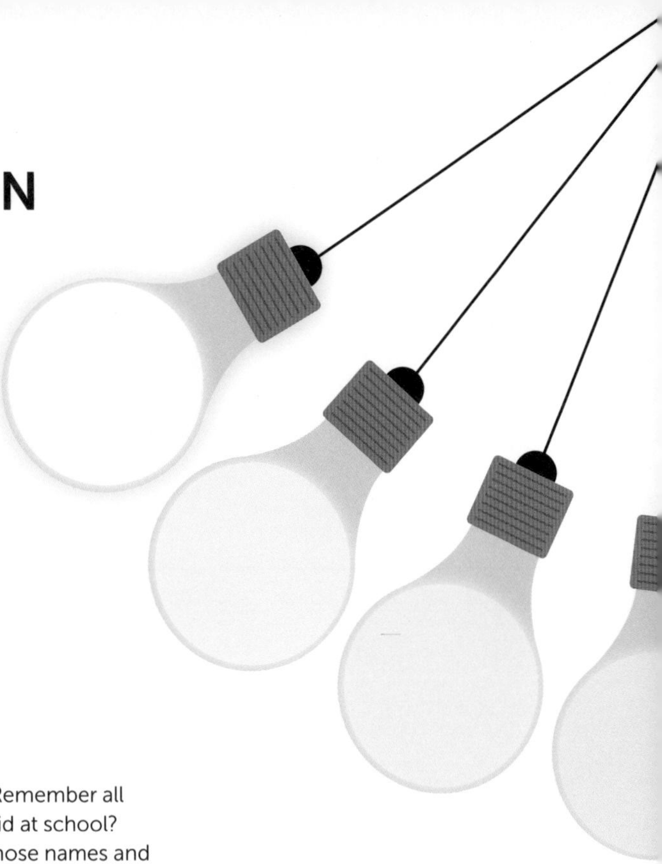

Thinking can be hard work. Remember all those maths problems you did at school? Remember memorizing all those names and dates for your history exam? It's not easy, thinking. It's a specific kind of activity, which philosophers who like their fancy words call 'epistemic labour'.

Occasionally, epistemic labourers are paid for their work. Published authors, for instance, are given money for thinking up thoughts and writing them down in books like this one. But thinking isn't the easiest thing to quantify, is it? *Is it?* By posing this question, we're asking you to perform a particular task – figuring out a solution – but is it the kind of task that can be measured in 'labour hours'? How much is your answer worth? This kind of vagueness, around quantity, quality and value, can mean that thinking isn't always construed as genuine labour. As such, it's not always properly paid for or even recognized. Understanding this is key to addressing certain asymmetries that appear in our everyday arguments.

When confronted by the testimony of victims – of office bullying, say, or institutional sexism and systemic racism – a common response is to ask: 'How can I help?'; 'What can I do?'; 'Tell me about your experience'. These are well-meaning questions, borne from a desire to improve an unjust situation. Unfortunately, they put the onus on the victims to do the work of providing an answer. As Audre Lorde puts it in *Age, Race, Class and Sex* (1995):

Let me tell you what it feels like to stand in front of a white man and explain privilege to him. It hurts. It makes you tired. Sometimes it makes you want to cry. Sometimes it is exhilarating. Every single time it is hard.

Black and Third-World people are expected to educate white people as to our humanity. Women are expected to educate men. Lesbian and gay men are expected to educate the heterosexual world. The oppressors maintain their position and evade their responsibility for their own actions . . .

The costs of explaining situations and thinking up solutions can be high – even higher when you're educating someone about your own suffering. In 'So Real It Hurts' (2011), Manissa McCleave Maharawal writes:

This is an example of what the American epistemologist Nora Berenstain calls 'epistemic exploitation'. It's a form of coerced labour that's typically unrecognized, largely uncompensated, and emotionally taxing to the point of being physically harmful. It's something we need to bear in mind when engaging in difficult discussions. Are we asking too much of our interlocutors? Are we asking them to relive trauma in order to provide evidence for it? If we're asking them to do all the epistemic labour, is that okay?

THINK FOR YOURSELF

Epistemic exploitation is a common phenomenon. In part, that's because it's perpetrated by people intent on 'doing the right thing'. These well-intentioned folk think they're 'just asking questions' or even 'exercising harmless curiosity'. There's a real possibility they might get angry at you if you accuse them of exploitation when they're 'just trying to help' – a phenomenon known as 'backlash'. These people, who exploit others, are people like us.

We exploit others without realizing, because epistemic exploitation is a crafty business. It often presents itself as neutral or even benevolent. It's hard to pin down. We can all too easily slip into asking someone else to think for us. 'Tell me . . .'; 'Can you explain . . . ?'; 'How is that even possible?'

Fortunately, there are moves we can make to avoid exploiting other people's epistemic labour.

The first thing to acknowledge, following the epistemologist Kristie Dotson, is that the testimonies that are often called for – descriptions of prejudice and oppression, say – already exist. They're out there, in books, magazines and online. Of course, as Dotson points out, the written words of the marginalized are often marginalized themselves – sidelined and suppressed, excluded from syllabuses and the mainstream media – and it can take an effort to learn the appropriate search terms (such as 'epistemic exploitation' and 'epistemic injustice').

Another way to address the problem is to try and disturb the concept of 'help'. 'How can I help?' is a loaded question. It's one-sided, since it suggests that the speaker exists in some way *outside* the problem. 'How can I help?' ignores the fact that systemic oppressions (racism, sexism, homophobia, ableism) are not simply problems for the people directly affected by them. Recent discussions about 'toxic masculinity' have demonstrated that men as well as women are affected by sexism and misogyny, albeit in different ways. There are, for instance, harmful and punishing standards of machismo to which men are expected to conform. One way for men to avoid shifting the burden of work onto women is for them to recognize they've got 'skin in the game' (for more on this, see our entry 'Solidarity').

Epistemic exploitation is an education issue. Those in privileged positions ask to be educated by those from marginalized groups – and this need could, and *should*, be met elsewhere. In addressing epistemic exploitation it pays to invest in public education. This is a central aim of recent attempts to 'decolonize the curriculum'. Looking at school and university syllabuses around the world, activists at the School of Oriental and African Studies (SOAS) in London saw a paucity of texts by scholars of colour: the curriculum was 'colonized'. It contained primarily white, male voices, talking about primarily white, male experiences of the world. This extends into secondary and primary school education as well – and the result is a gap in public knowledge about the experiences of, and theories developed by, people of colour. Bolstering our education systems will help us avoid epistemic exploitation. A useful question, then, that we should all ask ourselves is: 'Why is my curriculum so white?'

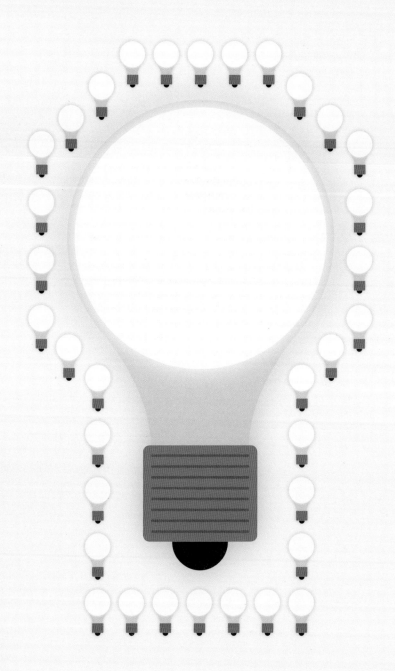

TOOLKIT

13

Allyship involves 'lending your voice' to others. Solidarity involves finding common cause with them. When disagreeing with others it's helpful to consider points of shared concern and whether you both have investment in the issue at hand.

14

Sometimes, common ground is found through simply spending time together. Views often shift slowly and indirectly, so eating with your interlocutor may be just as effective as restating your argument.

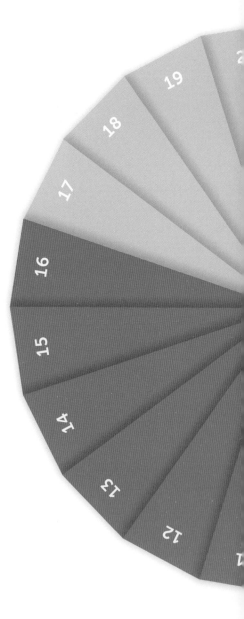

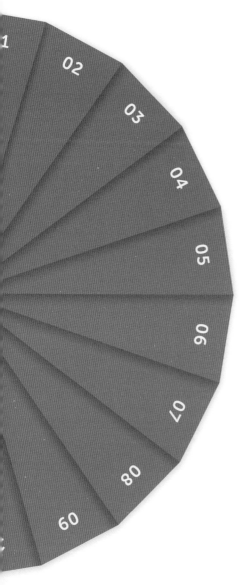

15

Humour creates boundaries that can exclude people or bring them closer together. When making jokes, consider the effect they have on the listeners. What shared assumptions are required for the jokes to work?

16

Thinking can be hard work, and difficult conversations can require a lot of 'epistemic labour'. It's important to consider who's doing the heavy lifting in a conversation. How else could the 'epistemic labour' be distributed and how can we improve our basic education?

FURTHER LEARNING

READ

White Fragility: Why It's So Hard for White People to Talk About Racism
Robin DiAngelo (Beacon Press, 2018)

London and the 1984–5 Miners' Strike
Edited by David Featherstone and Diarmaid Kelliher (2018)

WATCH

Dwelling Together. Directed by Meghna Gupta, this YouTube film documents a 2017 project organized by Darren Chetty and Abigail Bentley, focused on exploring multiculturalism, racism and identity.

The 2014 film *Pride*, directed by Matthew Warchus, tells the true story of solidarity between lesbian and gay activists and Welsh miners during the 1984 miners' strike.

LISTEN

The racistsandwich.com podcast, founded by Soleil Ho and Zahir Janmohamed, offers up in-depth discussions about the intersections between food and politics.

VISIT

London's MayDay Rooms is an educational charity set up to safeguard archival material about collaborative social movements and political solidarity. The Rooms run regular events, exploring radical ways of disagreeing.

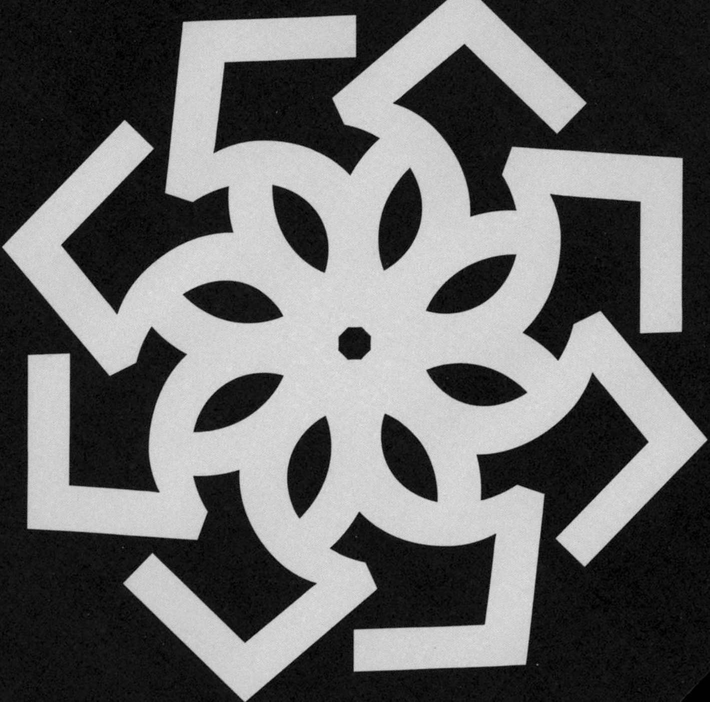

MOVING FORWARD

SECTIONS

'Rolling eyes = feminist pedagogy'
Sara Ahmed

Philosophy books can be deceptive. Open a philosophy book and you'll find a bunch of arguments laid out neatly on a page. 'X says this', 'Y says that', 'The perennial question about Z is such and such'. And so on. It's easy to be tricked into thinking that arguments just float around in the everlasting ether – that thoughts can drift free of context. Don't be fooled. They can't. Talking about talking in the abstract is a confusion, because even with our heads in the clouds our conversations take place in the world.

Think about the last argument you had. Did it unfold in some nonsensical, dimensionless 'nowhere' land? Chances are it was shouted out over a kitchen table, or muttered angrily down a telephone, or grumbled on the top-deck of the bus. Conversations, controversial or mundane, exist in our daily lives. And while it may be impossible to examine all the various uncomfortable encounters we run into, this chapter foregrounds specific 'real world' scenarios and examines how environment affects argument. Thinking about these literal and metaphorical spaces offers up methods for 'moving things forward', and we'll explore ways to shift gears in difficult conversations.

In section 17, 'New Spaces', the topic under discussion is veganism. How are conversations about veganism, vegetarianism and carnism affected by the spaces they appear in? Will it play out differently in an abattoir as opposed to a vegan restaurant? The physical location of a conversation clearly affects the participants' attitudes – but how?

Section 18, 'The Power of Questions', looks at the mechanics of questioning, and how a well-placed query can move conversations into less stuffy environs. A question is a tool which serves multiple purposes – it can elicit information, but it can put people at their ease as well. Here we'll look at an argument about the climate crisis, and consider how questions can help a dialogue to flourish.

In section 19, 'Taking Time', we revisit a theme discussed in the entry 'Going Slowly'. We look at the frenetic, almost uncontrollable speed with which arguments progress on social networking sites, and explore the possible virtues of a position called 'slow philosophy' in relation to the debate about euthanasia.

In the final section of the book we'll look at 'Self-Care'. Sometimes – not always, but *sometimes* – conversations simply aren't worth having. The emotional and psychological toll of talking to people intent on undermining you is too great, and the best thing to do is walk away. Here, we examine the costs of conversations about the social system known as white supremacy, and the political and personal utility in avoiding such discussions.

All too often, arguments flounder, or get stuck in unhelpful ruts. In this chapter, you'll find tactics for switching things up and moving things forward.

NEW SPACES

It's easy to argue about food. You can argue about how to prepare it (what's the best way to cook jollof rice?) and about what tastes nasty or nice (Marmite, anyone?). You can argue about the cultural, religious, ethical, aesthetic and health dimensions of what you eat – so despite the possible benefits of 'meal-sharing' (as seen in section 14), it's unsurprising that communal meals can be a source of disagreement if not downright discomfort.

Consider the following encounter. Mae, a long-time vegan, is visiting her family. She's dreading it. Every time she goes, her parents spend ages preparing a huge dinner based on the family's traditional Caribbean recipes: callaloo, pepperpot, roast pork and prawns in abundance. And every time she visits they have an argument about what she will and won't eat. And every time, she and her mum, Alvita, end up saying exactly the same things.

Mae: You know I can't eat this! I don't eat meat! I've told you a thousand times, I don't eat any kind of animal product. I've made a choice – I don't want to support food industries that are based on the systematic killing of living creatures. Animals aren't a *resource*, they're sentient beings who feel pain.

Alvita: Don't be so fussy! You know this is a family tradition. And this isn't just any old junk food – these dishes are part of who you are. This is the food your grandparents ate, and their parents before them. It's your history. It's your cultural heritage. It's part of your identity and your family's identity.

This is a fictional scenario and conversations rarely play out in so clear and explicit a fashion. The core disagreement, however, is a familiar one.

On the one hand, Mae is advancing an ethical argument grounded in a concern for animal welfare. Like the ethicists Carol J. Adams and Peter Singer, she thinks all suffering is morally relevant, irrespective of species. Meat-eating as it figures in the food industry is premised on the instrumentalizing and mass-killing of sentient creatures. So are the dairy and egg industries. Mae doesn't think the tasty pay-off is worth the pain. It's a 'utilitarian calculation', where she weighs up possible happiness against possible suffering and sees veganism to be the most morally justifiable response.

Alvita, on the other hand, is arguing that these dishes have important cultural significance. In talking about the relevance of food to their Caribbean heritage, Alvita aligns herself with writers like Cathryn Bailey and Ruby Tandoh, who recognize the deep and meaningful ways in which what we eat constructs our identities. Bailey argues that this may be particularly important for marginalized communities whose culinary heritages are sometimes ways of marking and addressing historical oppressions.

Both Mae and Alvita make good points, which is why such arguments are so difficult to resolve. How can they productively move forward?

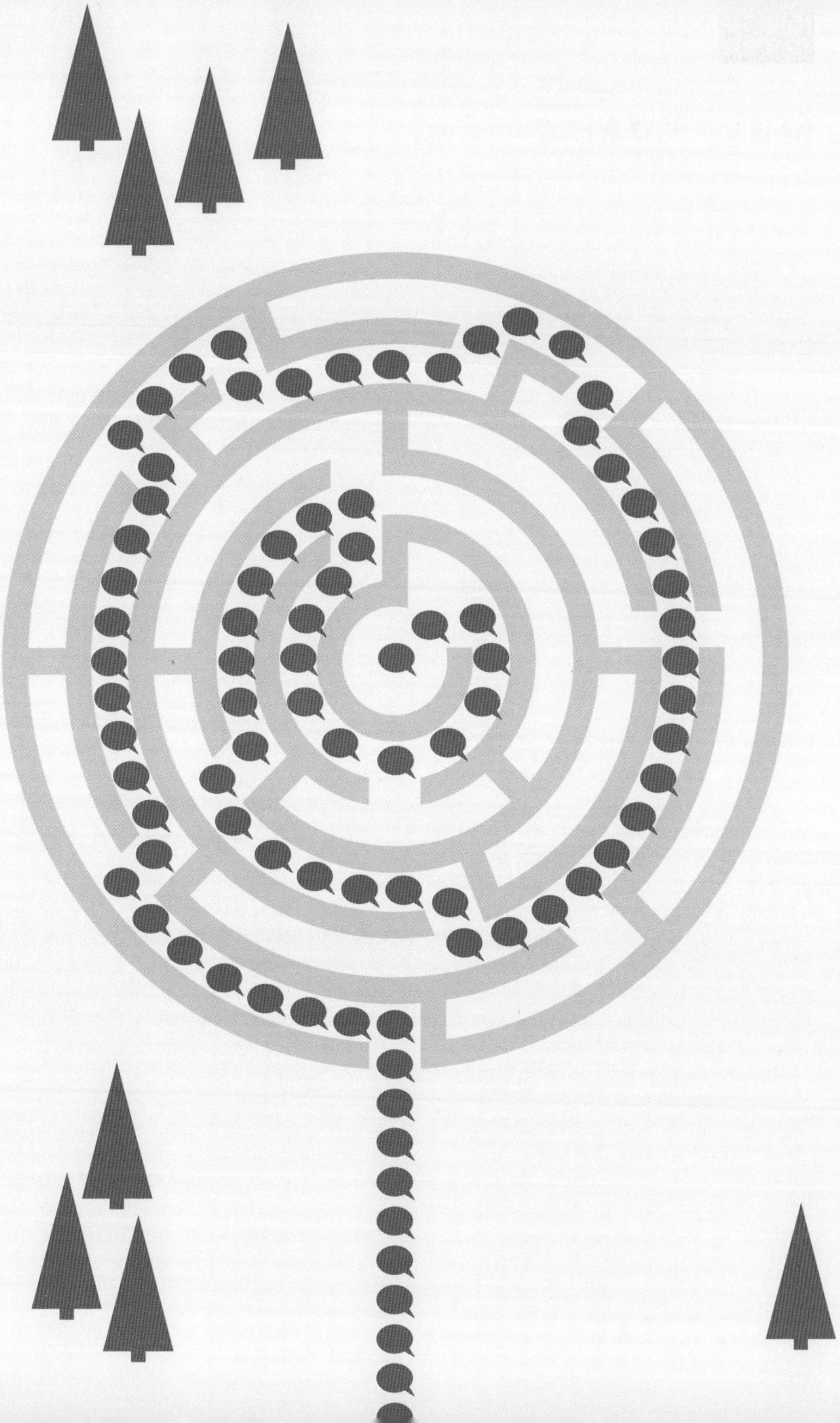

COMPANIONSHIP

Obviously, mealtimes can be a great opportunity to get together, catch up and have fun. Dining spaces, however, are not neutral spaces – and *place* has a huge role to play in how arguments, discussion and dialogue develop.

Think, for instance, how different it feels to argue in the privacy of your own home and on the top-deck of a bus. What about in a classroom and at the pub? Think about the relationship of the different people to the space you're inhabiting. Who feels comfortable there and how does that affect what they do and don't say?

When Mae visits her mum and dad, she enters a space where her parents 'set the rules'. It's the family home, and she's the child, and certain power dynamics result. Some practices are seen to be normal (eating meat, for instance). Others (veganism) are not. Behaviour is regulated, specific family scripts are performed, and all of this affects what Mae does and how her veganism is construed. There is much less chance that she will be accused of being 'fussy' in a vegan restaurant where she's paying for the meal.

Where you are can play almost as much of a role in how arguments develop as *what you say*.

It's also helpful to recognize the relevance of place for Alvita's argument. Markers of heritage can, as Bailey points out, achieve a particular importance for minority immigrant communities – especially when these communities are marginalized by wider society. While callaloo may not be regular fare in every British household, it is in Alvita's. Traditions can nurture feelings of belonging, which are important to immigrants and other marginalized people. These arguments, then, may have a very different resonance in the Caribbean.

A family dinner may well not be the best place for this argument. Greater understanding might be generated, not through any particular argumentative strategy, but rather by a literal change in location. A request to 'take the argument outside' might sound like an invitation to a fight – but getting a change of scene may well be sound advice.

The power of *place* is discussed and developed by French theorists Henri Lefebvre and Michel Foucault in works like *The Production of Space* (1974) and *Discipline and Punish* (1975). In the former, Lefebvre argues that our thinking is profoundly affected by the architectures that surround us; and in the latter, Foucault demonstrates how the affective dimension of space (the way space *affects* us) can be used as a way of exerting political and social control. *Where you are* can constrain your thoughts and determine what you think is possible.

The argument between Mae and Alvita may never be 'solved', but a change in location may lead to greater understanding. A trip to a vegan restaurant might not make Alvita think any differently about the cultural importance of home-cooked food, but it may help her see things from Mae's perspective.

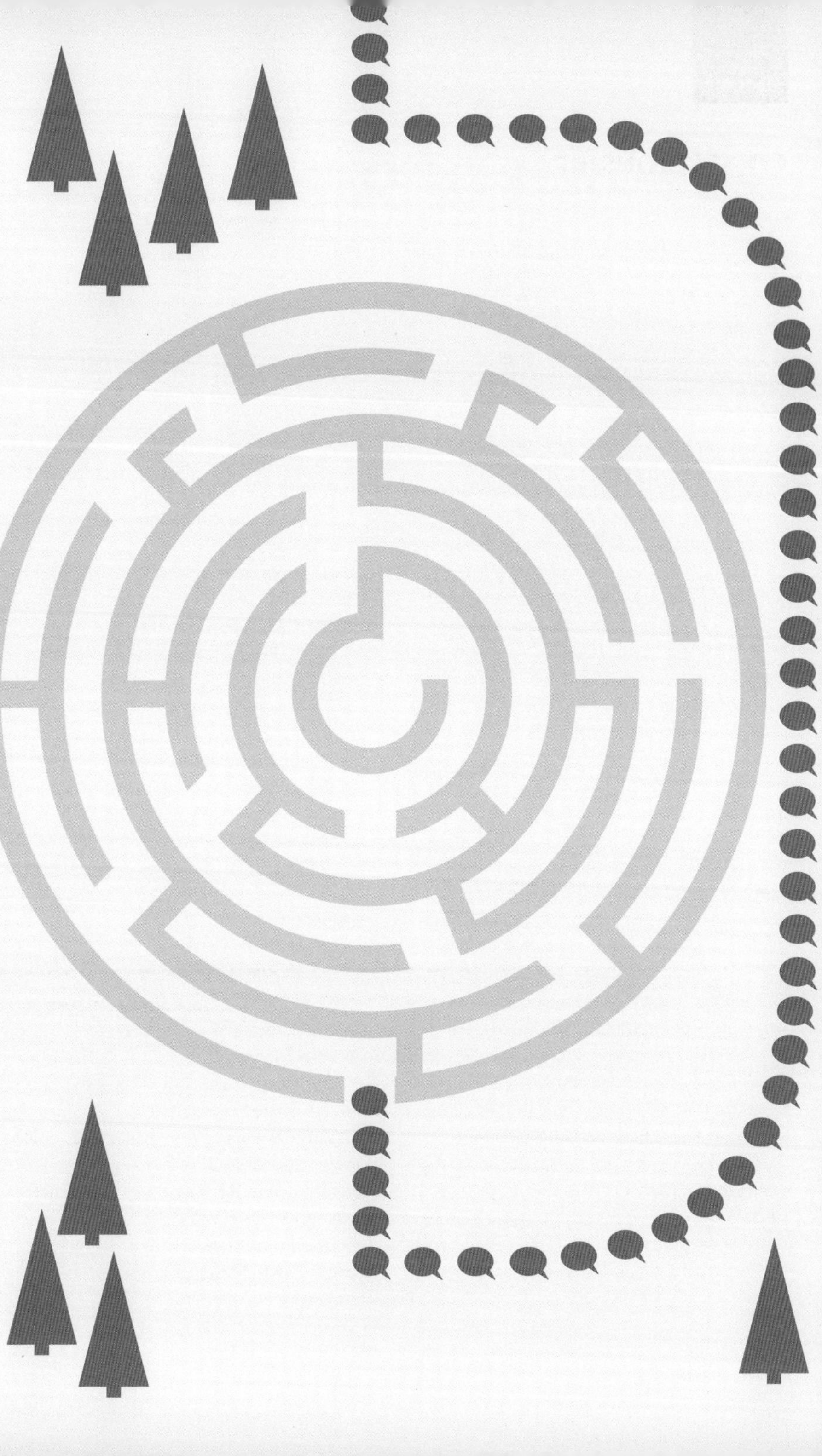

THE POWER OF QUESTIONS

A question is a tool that can be used for multiple purposes. That, at least, is the view advanced by the epistemologist Lani Watson in her paper 'Curiosity and Inquisitiveness' (2018). Watson says we use questions to get information, to communicate with one another, to express concern, to express *ourselves*, to make a noise – and many other things besides.

Consider the following scenario. You're sitting in your office and a co-worker walks in and loudly declares that they've just booked a flight to Barbados, adding, 'I don't care about this climate change stuff!'

Maybe, like your co-worker, you think the climate change debate is just a lot of hot air. Maybe you nod and go about your business. Unfortunately, the scientific evidence overwhelmingly suggests that global warming is a very real and very dangerous environmental phenomenon. The IPCC (Intergovernmental Panel on Climate Change) has issued repeated warnings about the effects of air travel on sea levels and it is becoming increasingly clear that as a planet we are in a worsening state of 'climate crisis'.

Given this, you may be troubled by your co-worker's comments. How do you react? Perhaps you decide it's best to keep quiet and mind your own business. Or maybe you feel compelled to interject?

'Are you being *serious?*' you ask. 'Don't you think the climate crisis is one of the most pressing issues of our time? Don't you know that unless we stop global warming, the sea levels will rise, there'll be mass flooding . . .'

In some ways, these questions aren't really questions at all. 'Are you being serious?' is a rhetorical device that implies your conversational partner can't actually be serious. Like 'Are you joking?' and 'Are you having a laugh?', it's intended to discredit them. Similarly, 'Don't you think . . . ?' isn't really a question. It's a way to state or restate your own position. You're not actually trying to find out what your interlocutor thinks, you're trying to tell them what you think – and perhaps to express horror that they don't think the same thing.

Hearing the scorn in your voice, your co-worker may be shamed into cancelling their flights. Perhaps they'll acknowledge the glibness of their remark and agree that global warming is not something to be spoken of so lightly. There's a chance, however, that your arch comments may make them more defensive and, having been criticized, they may 'double down' on their original position. Using these kinds of non-questions is a risky strategy. Horror and scorn are not inevitably going to encourage productive dialogue.

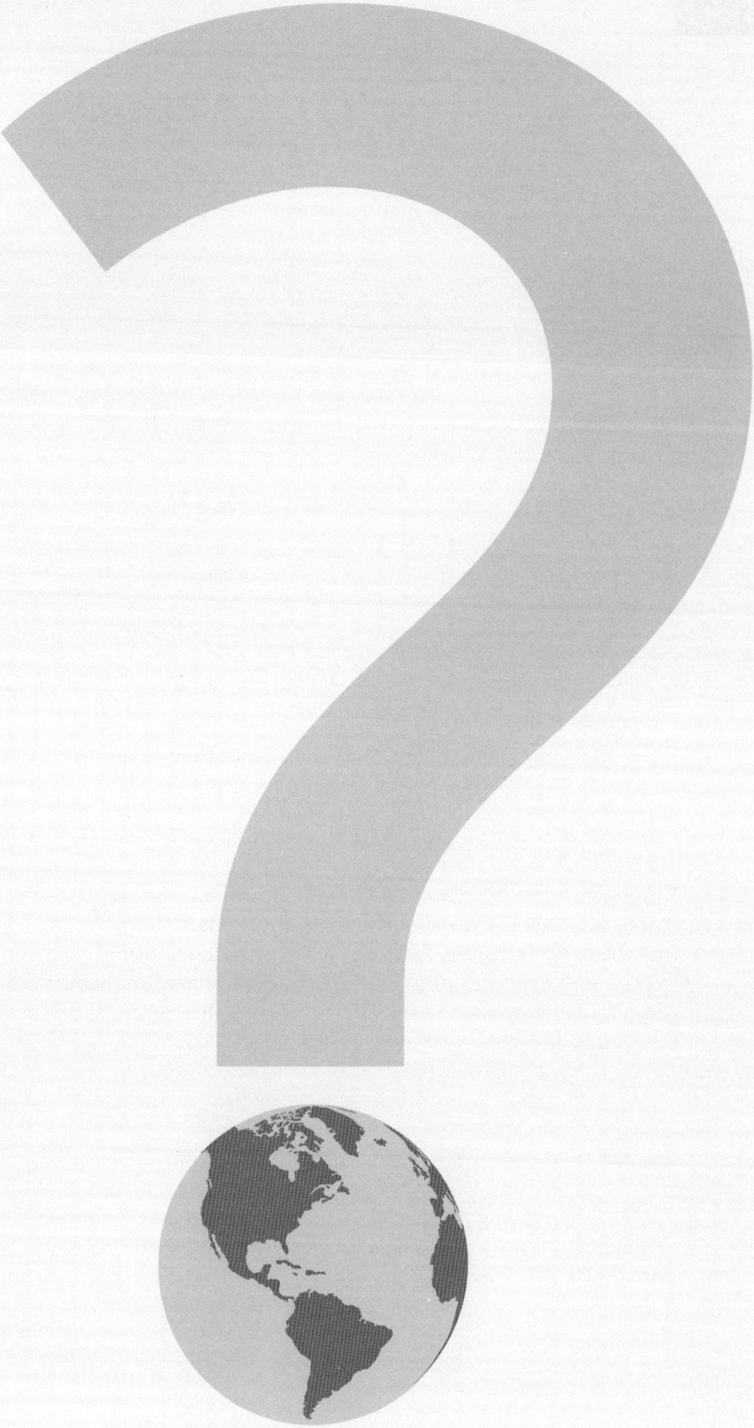

'CAN YOU TELL ME MORE?'

Some questions can have a positive outcome and foster understanding. In their article '"No Go Areas": Racism and Discomfort in the Community of Inquiry' (2016), Darren Chetty and Judith Suissa hone in on one question in particular: 'Can you tell me more?'

If the conversation with your co-worker becomes difficult or uncomfortable, 'Can you tell me more?' might help you gain a greater understanding. Instead of asking if they're 'being serious' (a non-question), you might ask them to tell you more about their views on climate change. It's an open, genuine invitation, and unlike the rhetorical 'Are you joking?', it generates knowledge. Your co-worker may, for instance, respond by telling you about their views on the racial politics of climate change discourse: 'A ban on air travel unfairly discriminates against immigrants who want to visit family in other countries. Global warming is a result of Western industrial history. Why should those who caused the problem – and who have already benefitted from these industrial advances – be allowed to ban other countries from doing the same thing?'

This is the kind of important information that can be elicited by the 'Can you tell me more?' question. And in contrast to 'Are you joking?', it demonstrates a readiness to listen, to 'stay in the conversation', as Lani Watson puts it. As such, the question fosters trust and reinforces the connection between the two speakers.

Chetty and Suissa also point out that 'Can you tell me more?' is crucially different to 'Why'-type questions. 'Unlike "why?", "can you tell me more?" is not a demand for justification.'

If, in response to your co-worker's initial comment, you were to hit them with a 'why' question – 'Why do you think that?' – you would be asking them to explain themselves. It's a coercive, high-minded approach, which positions you as the person to whom your co-worker is answerable. And while it's clearly important for such claims to be investigated, 'Can you tell me more?' is considerably more open, and will therefore generate more information and be less likely to lead to confrontation.

The asking of a genuine question also creates a greater parity between speakers. You may want your co-worker to explain themselves. You might equally be tempted, yourself, to explain why they're wrong to have been so dismissive about climate change. As Chetty and Suissa indicate, to do so is to create another asymmetrical power relation; you are positioning yourself as 'in the know'. Your co-worker is being positioned as someone to be 'educated'.

When asking questions, a good 'heuristic' (rule of thumb) is to consider whether you understand your partner's position well enough to repeat it back in a way that would satisfy them. This is a useful principle with which to organize the questions that you ask. You need to gather enough information before you rush to judgement and 'Can you tell me more?' allows you to do this, while also demonstrating trust, solidarity and a willingness to participate.

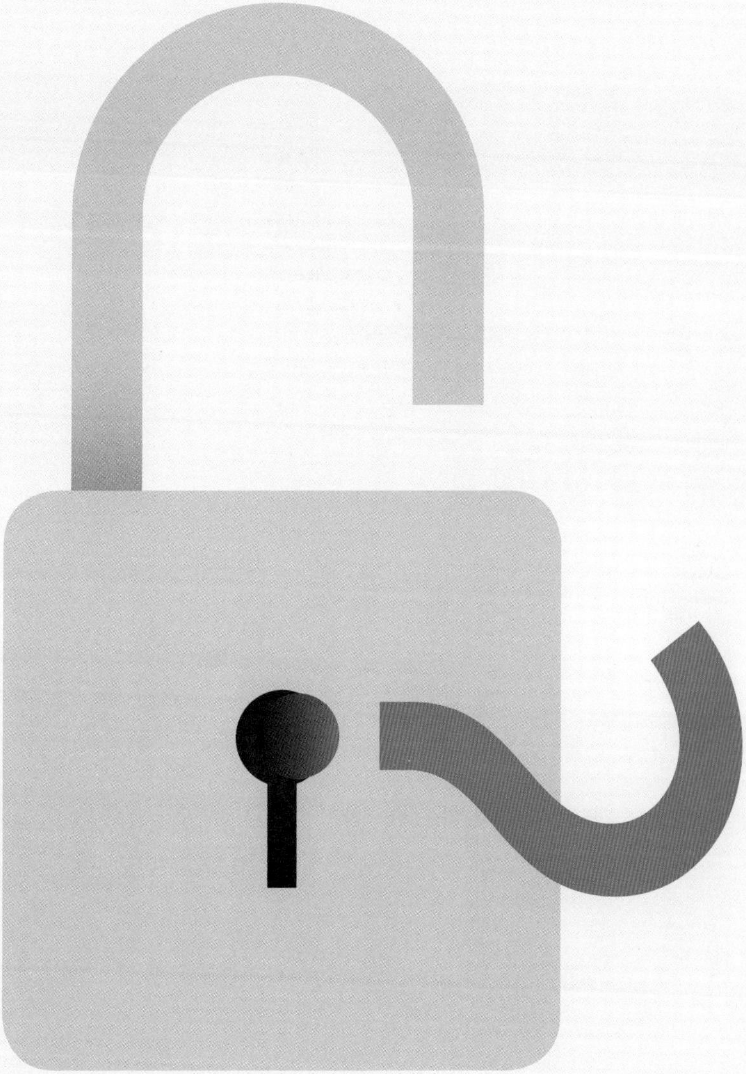

SOCIAL ME
VAST, FRE
CONVERSA
NETWORKS

A CREATES
ETIC
ONAL

TAKING TIME

These days, virtually everyone talks . . . virtually. A huge number of our conversations take place on social networking sites like Facebook, Twitter, Instagram and YouTube. And they're amazing. At the press of a button or swipe of a screen you can bundle your thoughts into tidy little packages and send them out into the infinite internet ether for millions to see and like and comment on.

Technologies like these have led to conversational networks with incredible potential. Looking, for instance, at the role social media played in the anti-government protests in the Middle East in 2010 (the 'Arab Spring'), ethicists like Marie-Luisa Frick have suggested that such sites can work as tools for powerful collective action. The internet will set us free . . . or so we tell ourselves.

It's not all roses, however. Sometimes it feels as if anything you say online runs the risk of a backlash, or at the very least a sarcastic cat video. Social networking sites are hotbeds of toxic disagreement, with users engaging in any number of fiery exchanges to the point of pure and pointless provocation (aka 'trolling').

A lot of sociologists think the violence of online disagreement is a function of the interface. Facebook and Twitter force us to interact in specific ways that often run counter to productive dialogue. The epistemologist C. Thi Nguyen encourages us to think about the phenomenon of 'echo chambers'. The algorithms that organize your 'news-feed' build on your online preferences and present you with information that reinforces your pre-existing beliefs rather than challenging them (creating 'echo chambers' and 'filter bubbles'). This – along with practices like 'defriending', where you silence voices you disagree with – leads to insularity and greater polarization of views (a problem touched on in section 14).

If that weren't enough, there's the frenetic pace of social media. How many friends do you have? How many followers? They're all posting comments and pictures, creating what the computer scientist Paul de Laat sees as a distinctly *hyperactive* style of communication, privileging quantity over quality. On top of this, we're constantly being bothered by pop-up adverts, harried by the 'ding' of incoming emails and tweets – and while the informational stream draws you in (it's designed to do so), it doesn't always foster careful analysis.

The worry, articulated by Shannon Vallor in 'Social Networking and Ethics' (2015), is that this emphasis on quantity rather than quality and this silencing of opposing voices damages the way we talk to one another. It frames conversations in ways that hamper 'deliberative public reason'. It allows us to converse, but not to foster understanding.

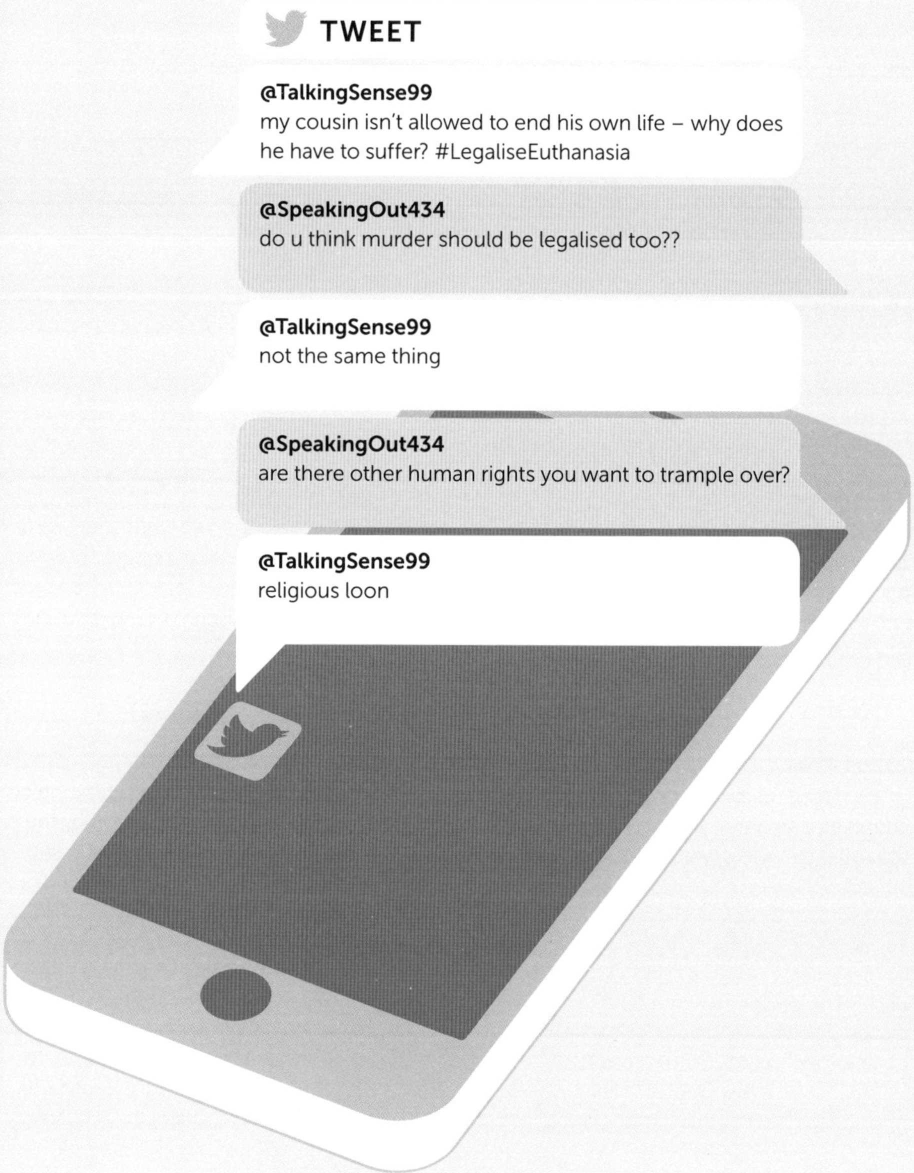
TWEET
@TalkingSense99
my cousin isn't allowed to end his own life – why does he have to suffer? #LegaliseEuthanasia
@SpeakingOut434
do u think murder should be legalised too??
@TalkingSense99
not the same thing
@SpeakingOut434
are there other human rights you want to trample over?
@TalkingSense99
religious loon

'TOO LONG, DIDN'T READ'

The busyness and breathtaking pace of the internet runs counter to what the philosopher Michelle Boulous Walker sees as the demand of 'slow' philosophy. Along with theorists like Maggie Berg and Barbara Seeber, Walker says we need to recognize the *temporality* of philosophical thought. Philosophy means the 'love of wisdom'; 'love' suggests care and attention. The point of philosophical engagement isn't to run through ideas, *bish bash bosh,* in order to come up with a quick-fix 'solution'. The point, says Walker, is to linger over thoughts, to contemplate, reflect and to complexify rather than simplify.

Think about chocolate. If you love chocolate, you don't just ram it in your mouth and quickly swallow. You *savour* it. You let it melt across your tongue. You try to figure out its various complex flavours. If you love it, you take time to appreciate its subtleties – and the same is true when you're engaged in philosophy. Walker quotes, admiringly, from Virginia Woolf's essay 'How Should One Read a Book?' (1925): 'Wait for the dust of reading to settle; for the conflict and questioning to die down; walk, talk, pull the dead petals from a rose, or fall asleep . . .'

Some will claim this ruminative approach is the preserve of those with disposable time and (by association) money. Not everyone can stroll about like a literary *flâneur,* aimlessly wandering the textual backstreets. Moreover, urgency is sometimes required (as we discuss in section 10). Bigoted remarks need to be called out. Action needs to be taken. It might even be that certain discussions should be blocked altogether, to avoid lending legitimacy to harmful viewpoints.

Yet there is still value in slowing down. Not everyone has the resources to engage in these online discussions, which is unfair and indicative of broader social ills, but those who *do* will benefit from interacting more thoughtfully. This doesn't have to mean years of careful study. It can be a matter of having a night to think something over, or a few extra minutes to read a blogpost. You'll get a better sense of an idea – and doing so may also make you less likely to leave a rash comment and be defensive. You may not have time to pull 'dead petals from a rose', but letting the proverbial dust settle, and resisting the allure of quick-fire responses, may indeed help you converse more productively.

TWEET

@SpeakingOut434
Hey @TalkingSense99 sorry I snapped back then.
sorry about your cousin 2

@SpeakingOut434
there are different reasons for thinking euthanasia's
wrong, but not all of them are religious

@SpeakingOut434
scholar-activist Harriet McBryde Johnson argues
that euthanasia is 'able-ist' (discriminates against
disabled people)

@SpeakingOut434
She points out that when a disabled person considers
euthanasia there's widespread agreement that their
choice is rational (their life 'isn't worth living')...

@SpeakingOut434
...but when an able-bodied person says the same
thing it's a 'tragedy' and every effort is made to
dissuade them from 'suicide'

@SpeakingOut434
why is it 'suicide' in one case and 'euthanasia' in
the other?

@SpeakingOut434
euthanasia leads to disabled people being helped to
commit suicide rather than provided with support that
could make their lives better

SELF-CARE

You can approach disagreements from a variety of angles. You can solicit a range of opinions, or address a background ignorance. You can move the conversation into another space, or shift the dialogue onto a different, more emotionally engaged register. You can do any number of things to improve an argument. Sometimes, however – and this is very important – you just have to walk away.

In 2017, the British journalist Reni Eddo-Lodge wrote a book titled *Why I'm No Longer Talking to White People About Race*. In it, she says: 'I'm no longer engaging with white people on the topic of race. Not all white people, just the vast majority who refuse to accept the legitimacy of structural racism and its symptoms.'

She describes a widespread pattern of behaviour, which she repeatedly experienced when talking with white people about race: the ways they deny the harmful effects of institutional racism and the failure to empathize with those suffering from those effects. She analyses how the educational work is laid at the feet of the marginalized, and examines the risks these conversations pose to people of colour, who need to tread carefully to avoid provoking racist tropes like those of the 'angry black person'. Faced with these obstacles, Eddo-Lodge made a decision to step back from these conversations.

It's this experience – of being repeatedly discredited, of being undermined and ignored – that Sara Ahmed examines in her

book *Living a Feminist Life* (2018). Ahmed talks about 'brick walls'. When engaging in dialogue we can 'come up against brick walls', and have the experience of 'hitting our heads against a wall'. It's a painful phenomenon – repeatedly banging into a hard, immovable object. 'The wall keeps its place,' writes Ahmed, 'so it is you that gets sore.' The institution of white supremacy holds hard and fast, and to hit it again and again can do damage.

Walls often appear in institutional contexts – the workplace or school – where someone is attempting to address or combat a problem with the status quo (in this case, systemic racism). The wall is a 'defence system', erected to prevent the questioning of 'normal' social structures, and it's experienced by some people but not others. 'You come up against what others do not see,' says Ahmed, 'and (this is even harder) you come up against what others are often invested in not seeing.' White people benefit from institutional racism so not only are they ignorant of its effects, they are invested in its upkeep.

It's painful and exhausting to engage in such conversations. It is draining to continually try and modify existing structures. These discussions are clearly important, but as Eddo-Lodge points out, they are also dangerous – for some participants more than others – and this makes it necessary to protect oneself. Sometimes walking away is the most sensible course of action.

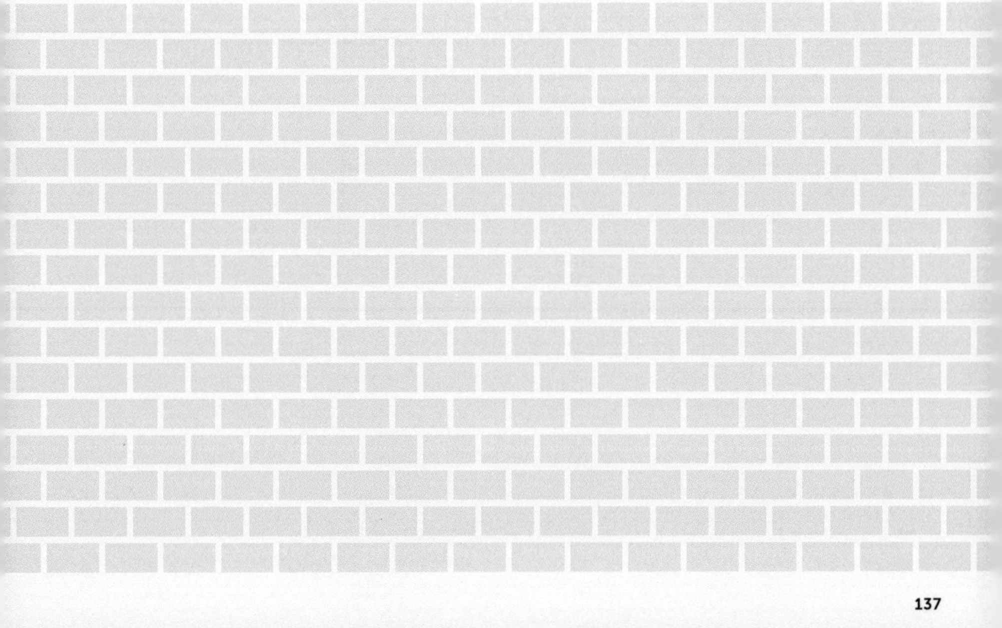

'TAKE CARE OF YOURSELF'

We live in societies riven by inequality. Do we have an obligation to stand up and call out unfair and prejudicial policies? To challenge wrongdoing? Do we have a responsibility to hold ourselves and others (including our governments) to account? On the whole, moral and political philosophers have argued that we do, but until recently few have examined how such obligations – the obligation to be 'engaged citizens', for instance – affect different people differently. Thinkers like Sara Ahmed and Reni Eddo-Lodge have demonstrated how some people run greater risks of 'activist burn-out' than others. The costs of political action are not the same for everyone. As a result, the idea of 'self-care' is becoming increasingly prominent in conversations about political action.

What is self-care? It's more than a soothing bubble-bath or a relaxing evening in with your favourite TV show. It's not just a matter of 'looking after yourself' and absenting yourself from boring political discourse. Self-care can, for some at least, figure itself as an act of resistance. This thought is articulated by the scholar-activist and poet Audre Lorde. In the epilogue to her essay collection *A Burst of Light* (1989), she writes: 'Caring for myself is not self-indulgence, it is self-preservation, and that is an act of political warfare.'

Resistance to a system of oppression is more than merely continued conversation and engagement ('fighting the good fight'). Resistance can be a matter of survival. Extending Lorde's thought, Ahmed says: 'When you are not supposed to live, as you are, where you are, with whom you are

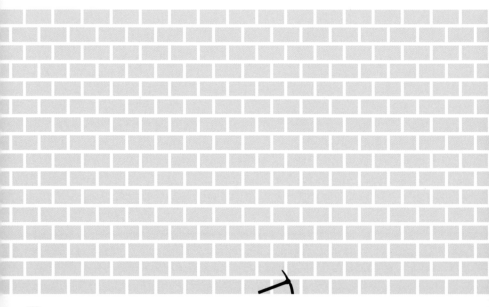

with, then survival is a radical action.' For the disenfranchised, self-care can be an act of resistance just as much as a spoken argument. The act of living in a homophobic society is a radical and dangerous act if you're gay, just as living in Nazi Germany was a radical and dangerous act for Jewish citizens.

Sometimes the best way to change minds might not be through conversation. You can respond to an argument by stepping away from it. In addition to self-care, withholding labour can be an important argumentative move as well – especially when you're being asked to bear too much of the conversational burden. In 2017, Eddo-Lodge announced she was going to stop talking to white people about race, and in doing so drew attention to the pervasiveness of structural racism. In 2016, Sara Ahmed resigned from her university post as a protest against institutional sexism and the reluctance on the part of her university to address it. Since 2016, feminist and pro-feminist activists have been organizing worldwide events known collectively as the 'International Women's Strike', in order to protest against widespread gender inequality. These are radical acts responding to ossified and unchanging debates.

For dialogue to be productive, certain things need to be in place. Where your interlocutor is unable or unwilling to listen, or to address their own ignorance, it makes sense to preserve your energies for other conversations. One of the greatest challenges in dialogue is determining whether the conditions necessary for 'productive disagreement' are actually present.

TOOLKIT

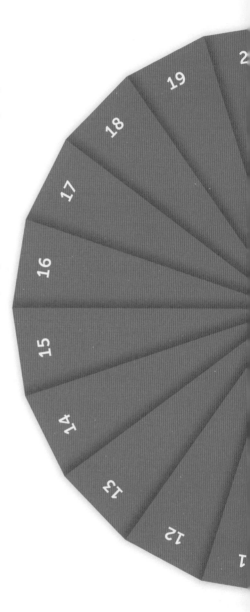

17

Where you are can play almost as much of a role in how disagreements play out as *what you say*. Consider the different factors contributing towards disagreement (place, tone of voice, history, etc.), and whether there's a better environment for this conversation to take place.

18

If someone says something offensive, it may be appropriate to withdraw from the conversation, but if you have the stamina, consider which questions might open up new avenues in the conversation.

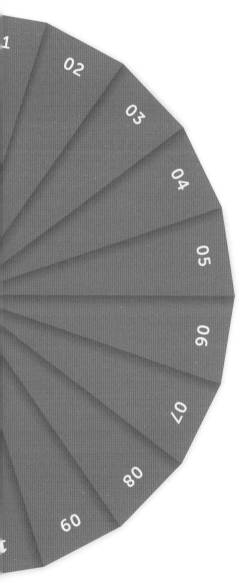

19

It's far too easy to get caught up in heated exchanges and to say things without properly thinking them through. Slowing the conversation down can help clarify a disagreement and make things more emotionally sustainable.

20

Occasionally, conversations will be too difficult to have. It's important to recognize how much energy you have to give. Consider what's at stake and what effect this conversation will have on your well-being. If it's too damaging, walk away.

FURTHER LEARNING

READ

***Why I'm No Longer Talking To White People
About Race***
Reni Eddo-Lodge (Bloomsbury, 2017)

WATCH

Do The Right Thing. Spike Lee's 1989
comedy-drama looks at an increasingly
confrontational disagreement between Italian
American and Black American residents of a
Brooklyn neighbourhood.

LISTEN

'When Civility is Used as a Cudgel Against
People of Color'. In this short instalment of
the American podcast Code Switch (NPR),
Karen Grigsby Bates looks at the ways that
'civility' is used to silence people of colour.

VISIT

Founded in 2015 and based in Sheffield,
the Festival of Debate consists of a series of
discussions, debates, Q&As and public talks
examining politics, economics and society.

EPILOGUE

Adam: We've finished! All our thoughts are out there in the world for people to read. How do you feel? Any regrets?

Darren: Well . . . yeah. There are moments when I read sections and imagine a reader saying, 'Ah! But have you thought about *x*?' Sometimes we have thought about *x* and have decided to leave it out for brevity's sake. And sometimes we won't have thought about *x* at all. So in a sense I regret that the book isn't more of a back-and-forth with the reader. How about you?

A: I regret everything! Always! But I'm pretty happy with how it's turned out. I hope we've left some nice trails of breadcrumbs for people to follow if they're interested. My main regret is neglecting certain topics. We debated a lot about whether to include discussions on Israel and Palestine, and trans rights – maybe we were overly cautious in leaving them out. Are there topics here that you think could make readers uncomfortable?

D: In the past, I've experienced people having their hackles raised by discussion of racism. I've experienced backlash too. But often, people who have stayed with these conversations and acknowledged their discomfort have changed their views.

A: It's easy to want to escape certain conversations. And sometimes that's fair enough – if a bigot is shouting at you, say. But, yeah, there's lots to gain from staying with a disagreement. Something I've noticed is that conversations can be much more productive when you live with your interlocutor. You're not as invested in having a generative conversation with strangers – you can go home afterwards and watch TV. If you're living with your interlocutor, the dynamic changes. If you disagree, you'd better disagree productively otherwise it's going to stay a problem.

D: I agree. In a relationship, for instance, there's a shared interest in the outcome of the conversation since there's a shared space, which both people inhabit. But doesn't that hold for other shared spaces too? Like the workplace? Maybe even the city? The world?! Aren't we still 'living with each other' in some sense?

A: Good point. I guess that's something we should think about in all our conversations. Am I actually invested in this argument? Or am I engaging with it like a game or a fight I can walk away from?

D: I think we're witnessing a rise in the idea of disagreement as spectacle. These days, public arguments are like game-shows. Political conversation has been reduced to a zero-sum game, where there's a Winner and a Loser. 'Heat' has become more important than 'light'. 'Heat', the anger, the combative style, is rewarded, generating the water-cooler moments and the shares on social media. I guess the best disagreements, while possibly containing moments of drama, aren't in all likelihood the best dramatic spectacles . . .

A: It certainly seems that way. And given the state of the world, and contemporary politics, it's easy to think things are only going to get worse.

D: I don't think that's inevitable. I think this book shows some helpful ways forward. I hope we've avoided the message that dialogue is the solution to all the world's problems, whilst keeping alive the idea of the possibility of productive disagreement.

A: Yeah, I guess so . . .

D: You don't sound convinced. Can you tell me more?

GLOSSARY

Argument An exchange in which people articulate opposing views. Alternatively (in logic), a series of premises leading towards a conclusion.

Capitalism An economic system in which private owners employ/exploit others in order to make profit in the marketplace.

Debate A form of argument in which opposing views are put forward and assessed (often with a vote). Participants 'win' if they successfully defend their original position.

Democracy A political system where decision-making is ultimately done by the public or 'demos'. 'Deliberative democracy' is a democratic mode that foregrounds public deliberation.

Despotism A type of government in which a single individual (a despot) rules with absolute power.

Dialogue A conversational exchange between two or more people.

Discourse Written or spoken communication.

Egalitarian A term used to describe the view that all people are equal and deserving of equal rights and opportunities.

Enlightenment A controversial term used to describe the period of intellectual development in the West in the seventeenth and eighteenth centuries.

Epistemology The branch of philosophy that deals with what we know and how we know it (from the Greek *'episteme'*, meaning 'knowledge').

Himpathy A blending of 'him' and 'sympathy' to describe inappropriate sympathy for male perpetrators of violence.

Metaphysics The branch of philosophy that examines the structure of reality and what things exist.

Misogyny The hatred of and/or ingrained prejudice against women.

Modernism An intellectual movement in the late nineteenth and early twentieth century which responded to the societal shifts caused by the Industrial Revolution.

No-platforming The practice by which individuals are denied the opportunity to speak on certain platforms.

Paternalism The policy, practice or attitude in which one group organizes the interests of those groups that are dependent upon them.

Patronization An attitude in which an individual or group patronizes – treats condescendingly – another.

Pedagogy The theory of teaching.

Post-modernism An intellectual movement characterized by its critique of Modernist notions of truth, rationality and reality.

Relativism The view that things like truth, beauty and goodness are relative to a frame of reference and not absolute.

Signal boosting A process by which political messages are amplified for a wider audience to hear.

Snowflake A term used to refer to apparently 'overly sensitive' individuals (who 'melt' at the slightest provocation).

Speech act A verbal utterance that both conveys information and performs an action.

Torpified subject Someone who has been paralysed by panic in the face of their own prejudices.

Totalitarianism A dictatorial system of government that demands citizens be totally subservient to the state.

White supremacy A political system that uses the concept of 'race' to systematically privilege and empower white people over everyone else.

NAMES AND SPELLING

Names are important and carry political weight. The philosopher bell hooks, mentioned in the text, has drawn attention to this with her use of lower-case lettering ('b' and 'h'). The same is true for Nathaniel Adam Tobias ~~Coleman~~, who strikes through 'Coleman' in recognition of the fact that it was the name given to their family by slave owners.

BIBLIOGRAPHY

Sara Ahmed, *Living a Feminist Life* (Duke University Press, 2018)

Linda Martín Alcoff, 'The Problem of Speaking for Others' (Cultural Critique, 1991)

Bhimrao Ambedkar, 'The Annihilation of Caste' (Undelivered Speech, 1936)

Kwame Anthony Appiah, *Cosmopolitanism: Ethics in a World of Strangers* (Norton, 2006)

Kwame Anthony Appiah, 'Liberalism, Individuality, and Identity' (Critical Inquiry, 2001)

Barbara Applebaum, *Being White, Being Good* (Lexington Books, 2010)

Hannah Arendt, *The Origins of Totalitarianism* (Schocken Books, 1951)

Cathyrn Bailey, 'We Are What We Eat: Feminist Vegetarianism and the Reproduction of Racial Identity' (Hypatia, 2007)

Zara Bain, 'Is There Such a Thing as "White Ignorance" in British Education?' (Ethics and Education, 2018)

Elizabeth Barnes, 'Valuing Disability, Causing Disability' (Ethics, 2014)

Simone de Beauvoir, *The Second Sex* (Alfred A Knopf Inc, 1949)

Seyla Benhabib, 'Feminism and Postmodernism: An Uneasy Alliance' (Feminist Contentions, 1998)

Nora Berenstain, 'Epistemic Exploitation' (Ergo, 2016)

Megan Boler, *Feeling Power: Emotions and Education* (Routledge, 1999)

Nicholas Burbules, 'Being Critical About Being Critical' (Democracy and Education, 2017)

Judith Butler, *Psychic Life of Power* (Stanford University Press, 1997)

Darren Chetty and Judith Suissa, '"No Go Areas": Racism and Discomfort in the Community of Inquiry' (*The Routledge International Handbook of Philosophy for Children,* 2016)

Ted Cohen, *Jokes: Philosophical Thoughts on Joking Matters* (University of Chicago Press, 1999)

Nathaniel Adam Tobias Coleman, *The Duty to Miscegenate* (PhD Dissertation, 2013)

Benjamin Constant, *Principles of Politics* (1815)

René Descartes, *Meditations on First Philosophy* (1641)

Ann Diller, 'Facing the Torpedo Fish' (Philosophy of Education, 1998)

Kristie Dotson, 'Between Rocks and Hard Places: Introducing Black Feminist Professional Philosophy' (The Black Scholar, 2016)

Reni Eddo-Lodge, *Why I'm No Longer Talking to White People About Race* (Bloomsbury, 2017)

Emmanuel Chukwudi Eze, 'The Color of Reason' (*Postcolonial African Philosophy: A Critical Reader,* 1997)

Frantz Fanon, *Black Skin, White Masks* (Éditions du Seuil, 1952)

Michel Foucault, *Discipline and Punish* (Gallimard, 1975)

Marie-Luisa Frick and Andreas Oberprantacher, 'Shared Is Not Yet Sharing, Or: What Makes Social Networking Services Public?' (International Review of Information Ethics, 2011)

Roxane Gay, 'On Making Black Lives Matter' (*Marie Claire,* 2016)

Jonathan Haidt and Greg Lukianoff, *The Coddling of the American Mind* (Penguin, 2018)

Georg Wilhelm Friedrich Hegel, *The Phenomenology of the Spirit* (1807)

bell hooks, *Teaching to Transgress* (Routledge, 1994)

Waheed Hussain, 'The Common Good' (*Stanford Encyclopaedia of Philosophy,* 2018)

Harriet McBryde Johnson, 'Unspeakable Conversations' (*The New York Times,* 2003)

Immanuel Kant, *Critique of Pure Reason* (1781)

Immanuel Kant, 'On the Different Races of Man' (1775)

Jamaica Kincaid, *A Small Place* (Farrar, Straus and Giroux, 2000)

Paul de Laat, 'Trusting Virtual Trust' (Ethics and Information Technology, 2006)

Robin Lakoff, 'The Logic of Politeness, Or: Minding Your P's and Q's' (Papers from the Ninth Regional Meeting of the Chicago Linguistics Society, 1973)

Rae Langton, *Sexual Solipsism* (Oxford University Press, 2009)

Henri Lefebvre, *The Production of Space* (Basil Blackwell, 1974)

Adam Lefstein, 'Dialogic Teaching: A New, Ancient Idea' (The Moshinsky Conference for School Principals, 2013)

Zeus Leonardo, *Race, Whiteness and Education* (Routledge, 2009)

Genevieve Lloyd, *The Man of Reason* (Methuen, 1984)

Audre Lorde, *A Burst of Light: and Other Essays* (Dover Publications, 1989)

Audre Lorde, 'Age, Race, Class and Sex' (Sister Outsider, 1984)

Maria Lugones, *Pilgrimages/Peregrinajes: Theorizing Coalition Against Multiple Oppressions* (Rowman and Littlefield, 2003)

Manissa McCleave Maharawal, 'So Real It Hurts' (Left Turn, 2011)

Herbert Marcuse, *One-Dimensional Man* (Beacon Press, 1964)

Vivian May, 'Trauma in Paradise' (Hypatia, 2006)

Nadia Mehdi, '"Just a Joke": On Joking and Oppression' (draft)

John Stuart Mill, *On Liberty* (John W. Park and Son, 1859)

Charles Mills, *The Racial Contract* (Cornell University Press, 1997)

Chantal Mouffe, *The Democratic Paradox* (Verso, 2000)

Chantal Mouffe, 'Deliberative Democracy or Agonistic Pluralism' (Reihe Politikwissenschaft, 2000)

C. Thi Nguyen, 'Echo Chambers and Epistemic Bubbles' (Episteme, 2019)

John Rawls, *Theory of Justice* (Belknap, 1971)

Phyllis Rooney, 'Philosophy, Adversarial Argumentation and Embattled Reason' (Informal Logic, 2010)

Amelie Oksenberg Rorty, 'Persons and Personae' (The Person and the Human Mind, ed. Gill, 1990)

Jean-Jacques Rousseau, *The Social Contract* (1762)

Naomi Scheman, 'Queering the Center by Centering the Queer' (Feminists Rethink the Self, ed. Meyers, 1997)

Madeleine de Scudéry, 'Of Politeness' (*Conversations nouvelles sur divers sujets*, 1684)

Rebecca Solnit, *Men Explain Things To Me, And Other Essays* (Haymarket Books, 2014)

Elizabeth Spelman, *Inessential Woman* (Beacon Press, 1988)

Gopal Sreenivasan, 'Understanding Alien Morals' (Philosophy and Phenomenological Research, 2001)

Ruby Tandoh, *Eat Up* (Serpent's Tail, 2018)

Deborah Tannen, *The Argument Culture* (Little Brown, 1998)

Joyce Trebilcot, 'Dyke Methods' (Hypatia, 1988)

Shelley Tremain, *Foucault and Feminist Philosophy of Disability* (University of Michigan Press, 2017)

Shannon Vallor, 'Social Networking and Ethics' (Stanford Encyclopaedia of Philosophy, 2015)

Michelle Boulous Walker, *Slow Philosophy* (Bloomsbury, 2016)

Lani Watson, 'Curiosity and Inquisitiveness' (*The Routledge Handbook of Virtue Epistemology*, 2018)

Moira Weigel, 'Review of "The Coddling of the American Mind"' (*Guardian*, 2018)

Mary Wollestonecraft, *A Vindication of the Rights of Women* (1792)

Virginia Woolf, 'How Should One Read A Book?' (*The Common Reader*, 1925)

BUILD +
BECOME

At BUILD+BECOME we believe in building knowledge that helps you navigate your world.

Our books help you make sense of the changing world around you by taking you from concept to real-life application through 20 accessible lessons designed to make you think. Create your library of knowledge.

Whether you lead a business of thousands, are at the start of your entrepreneurial journey, or are a professional, teacher, parent or student, Conscious Leadership challenges you to be aware, awake and connected as you boldly take on your future.

In 20 proactive lessons – each including powerful practices and exercises – Neil Seligman provides you with the essential tools to increase your emotional intelligence, build stress-resilience and lead yourself and others with greater compassion, clarity and joy.

Neil Seligman is a an international mindfulness advocate, conscious visionary and author. He is the Founder of The Conscious Professional, the author of *100 Mindfulness Meditations* and the originator of Soul Portrait Photography. Neil specializes in delivering inspiring keynotes, workshops and seminars on Conscious Leadership, mindfulness and resilience to busy professionals. www.theconsciousprofessional.com.

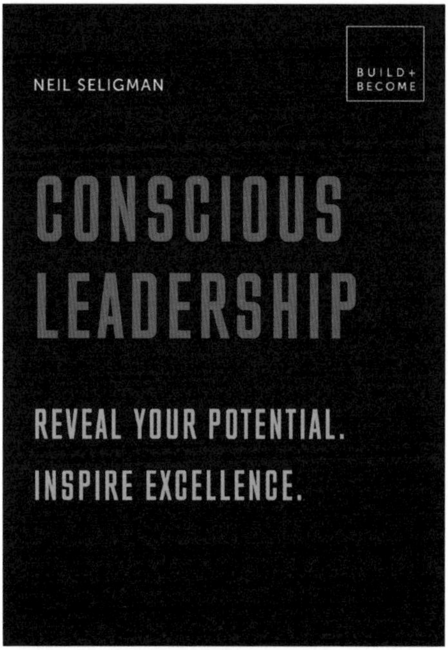
NEIL SELIGMAN
BUILD+ BECOME
CONSCIOUS LEADERSHIP
REVEAL YOUR POTENTIAL.
INSPIRE EXCELLENCE.

BE THE CHANGE.

Using a unique, visual approach, Gerald Lynch explains the most important tech developments of the modern world – examining their impact on society and how, ultimately, we can use technology to achieve our full potential.

From the driverless transport systems hitting our roads to the nanobots and artificial intelligence pushing human capabilities to their limits, in 20 dip-in lessons this book introduces the most exciting and important technological concepts of our age, helping you to better understand the world around you today, tomorrow and in the decades to come.

Gerald Lynch is a technology and science journalist, and is currently Senior Editor of technology website TechRadar. Previously Editor of websites Gizmodo UK and Tech Digest, he has also written for publications such as *Kotaku* and *Lifehacker*, and is a regular technology pundit for the BBC. Gerald was on the judging panel for the James Dyson Award. He lives with his wife in London.

GERALD LYNCH

BUILD + BECOME

GET TECHNOLOGY

BE IN THE KNOW.
UPGRADE YOUR FUTURE.

KNOW TECHNOLOGY TODAY, TO EQUIP YOURSELF FOR TOMORROW.

Using a unique, visual approach to explore philosophical concepts, Adam Ferner shows how philosophy is one of our best tools for responding to the challenges of the modern world.

From philosophical 'people skills' to ethical and moral questions about our lifestyle choices, philosophy teaches us to ask the right questions, even if it doesn't necessarily hold all the answers. With 20 dip-in lessons from history's great philosophers alongside today's most pioneering thinkers, this book will guide you to think deeply and differently.

Adam Ferner has worked in academic philosophy both in France and the UK, but much prefers working outside the academy in youth centres and other alternative learning spaces. He is the author of *Organisms and Personal Identity* (2016) and has published widely in philosophical and popular journals. He is an associate editor of the Forum's *Essays,* and a member of Changelings, a North London fiction collaboration.

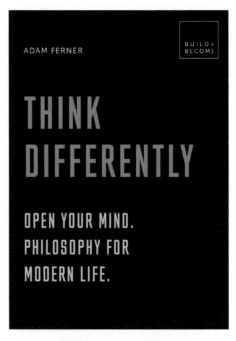

ADAM FERNER

BUILD+ BECOME

THINK DIFFERENTLY

OPEN YOUR MIND. PHILOSOPHY FOR MODERN LIFE.

PHILOSOPHY IS ABOUT OUR LIVES AND HOW WE LIVE THEM.

Using a unique, visual approach to explore the science of behaviour, *Read People* shows how understanding why people act in certain ways will make you more adept at communicating, more persuasive and a better judge of the motivations of others.

The increasing speed of communication in the modern world makes it more important than ever to understand the subtle behaviours behind everyday interactions. In 20 dip-in lessons, Rita Carter translates the signs that reveal a person's true feelings and intentions and exposes how these signals drive relationships, crowds and even society's behaviour. Learn the influencing tools used by leaders and recognize the fundamental patterns of behaviour that shape how we act and how we communicate.

Rita Carter is an award-winning medical and science writer, lecturer and broadcaster who specializes in the human brain: what it does, how it does it, and why. She is the author of *Mapping the Mind* and has hosted a series of science lectures for public audience. Rita lives in the UK.

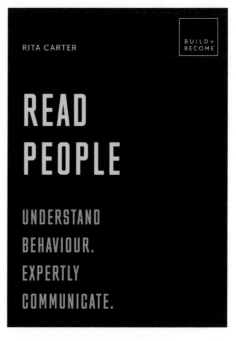

RITA CARTER

BUILD + BECOME

READ PEOPLE

UNDERSTAND BEHAVIOUR. EXPERTLY COMMUNICATE.

CAN YOU SPOT A LIE?

Using a unique, visual approach, Nathalie Spencer uncovers the science behind how we think about, use and manage money to guide you to a wiser and more enjoyable relationship with your finances.

From examining how cashless transactions affect our spending and decoding the principles of why a bargain draws you in, through to exposing what it really means to be an effective forecaster, *Good Money* reveals how you can be motivated to be better with money and provides you with essential tools to boost your financial wellbeing.

Nathalie Spencer is a behavioural scientist at Commonwealth Bank of Australia. She explores financial decision making and how insights from behavioural science can be used to boost financial wellbeing. Prior to CBA, Nathalie worked in London at ING where she wrote regularly for *eZonomics*, and at the RSA, where she co-authored *Wired for Imprudence: Behavioural Hurdles to Financial Capability*, among other titles.

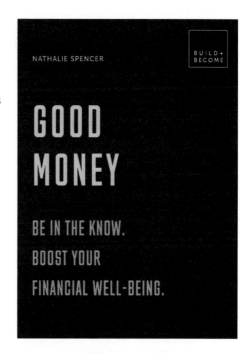

NATHALIE SPENCER

BUILD + BECOME

GOOD MONEY

BE IN THE KNOW.
BOOST YOUR
FINANCIAL WELL-BEING.

WE ALL MAKE CHOICES
WITH MONEY –
UNDERSTAND YOURS.

Through a series of 20 practical and effective exercises, all using a unique visual approach, Michael Atavar challenges you to open your mind, shift your perspective and ignite your creativity. Whatever your passion, craft or aims, this book will expertly guide you from bright idea, through the tricky stages of development, to making your concepts a reality.

We often treat creativity as if it was something separate from us – in fact it is, as this book demonstrates, incredibly simple: creativity is nothing other than the very core of 'you'.

Michael Atavar is an artist and author. He has written four books on creativity – *How to Be an Artist, 12 Rules of Creativity, Everyone Is Creative* and *How to Have Creative Ideas in 24 Steps – Better Magic.* He also designed (with Miles Hanson) a set of creative cards *'210CARDS'*.

He works 1-2-1, runs workshops and gives talks about the impact of creativity on individuals and organizations. www.creativepractice.com

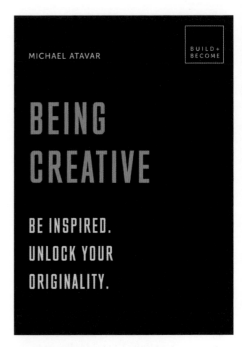

MICHAEL ATAVAR

BUILD + BECOME

BEING CREATIVE

BE INSPIRED. UNLOCK YOUR ORIGINALITY.

CREATIVITY BEGINS WITH YOU.

We are living longer than ever and, thanks to technology, we are able to accomplish so much more. So why do we feel time poor? In 20 eye-opening lessons, Catherine Blyth combines cutting-edge science and psychology to show why time runs away from you, then provides the tools to get it back.

Learn why the clock speeds up just when you wish it would go slow, how your tempo can be manipulated and why we all misuse and miscalculate time. But you can beat the time thieves. Reset your body clock, refurbish your routine, harness momentum and slow down. Not only will time be more enjoyable, but you really will get more done.

Catherine Blyth is a writer, editor and broadcaster. Her books, including *The Art of Conversation* and *On Time*, have been published all over the world. She writes for publications including the *Daily Telegraph*, *Daily Mail* and *Observer* and presented *Does Happiness Write White?* for Radio 4. She lives in Oxford.

CATHERINE BLYTH

BUILD + BECOME

ENJOY TIME

STOP RUSHING.
GET MORE DONE.

TIME IS NOT MONEY.
TIME IS YOUR LIFE.

Mathematics is an indispensable tool for life. From the systems that underpin our newsfeeds, through to the data analysis that informs our health and financial decisions, to the algorithms that power how we search online — mathematics is at the heart of how our modern world functions.

In 20 dip-in lessons, *Understanding Numbers* explains how and why mathematics fuels your world and arms you with the knowledge to make wiser choices in all areas of your life.

Rachel Thomas and **Marianne Freiberger** are the editors of *Plus* magazine, which publishes articles from the world's top mathematicians and science writers on topics as diverse as art, medicine, cosmology and sport (plus.maths.org).

Rachel and Marianne have co-authored the popular maths books *Numericon* and *Maths Squared*, and were editors on *50: Visions of Mathematics*. Between them they have nearly 30 years of experience writing about mathematics for a general audience.

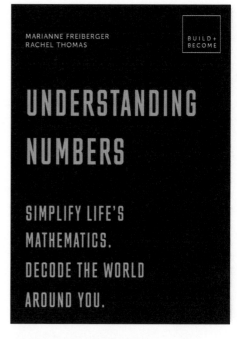

MARIANNE FREIBERGER
RACHEL THOMAS

BUILD + BECOME

UNDERSTANDING NUMBERS

SIMPLIFY LIFE'S MATHEMATICS. DECODE THE WORLD AROUND YOU.

MATHEMATICS IS AT THE HEART OF OUR WORLD.

ACKNOWLEDGEMENTS

Commissioning Editor Lucy Warburton
Editor Emma Harverson
Copyeditor Rachel Malig
Readers Shantel Edwards, Nadia Mehdi and Ruby Tandoh
Design and illustration Transmission

First and foremost, we would like to thank our excellent editors and awesome readers. We would also like to thank our friends and colleagues, particularly Christian Albert, Zara Bain, Anna Bennett, Abigail Bentley, Sam Berkson, Emily Berry, Chris Beschi, Jack Bicker, Jeffrey Boakye, Kim Bonnar, Florence Bullough, Jason Buckley, Kit Caless, Ben Chijioke, Nenna Chuku, Fen Coles, James Cox, Maeve Duval, Elianna Fetterolf, the Ferners, Alice Franklin, Niki Fitzgerald, Kathy Gale, Greggs, Maughn Gregory, Meghna Gupta, Medi Gwosdz, Joshua Habgood-Coote, Beth Hannon, Joanna Haynes, Mya Kalaya, Diarmaid Kelliher, Walter Omar Kohan, Bréanainn Lambkin, Grace Lockrobin, Lottie Manzi, Luke Massey, Michael Merry, Chris Meyns, Jonathan Nassim, Rachel Rosen, Laurencia Saenz Benavides, Mike Smith, Judith Suissa, Will Tattersdill, Liza Thompson, Graeme Tiffany, Patrick Turner, Lou Tyson, Vivienne Watson, Andy West, Steve Williams, Peter Worley, Sapere, The Good Immigrant contributors, The Dwelling Together participants, The UK HipHopEd regulars, The Reflecting Realities Steering Committee, The Changelings and The Mankind Group at Platform.

Above all, we would like to thank Rageshri Dhairyawan and Esther McManus, who made this book possible (and much else besides).

Adam Ferner completed his PhD in 2012 and has worked in academic philosophy both in France and the UK. These days, he much prefers working outside the academy in youth centres and other alternative learning spaces, and his present research focuses on ways of opening up philosophy to new audiences. He has published widely in philosophical and popular journals and has written three books, *Organisms and Personal Identity* (Routledge, 2016), *Think Differently* (White Lion Publishing, 2018) and – with Nadia Mehdi and Zara Bain – *Crash Course: Philosophy* (Ivy, 2019). He is co-writing his fifth book, *Philosophical Empires*, with Chris Meyns, forthcoming in 2020. Adam is an associate editor of the Forum's *Essays*, and a member of the Changelings, a North London fiction collaboration.

Darren Chetty has published academic work on philosophy, education, racism, children's literature and hip-hop culture. He is a contributor to the bestselling book, *The Good Immigrant*, edited by Nikesh Shukla (Unbound 2016). Darren is co-author, with Jeffrey Boakye, of *What Is Masculinity? Why Does It Matter? And Other Big Questions* (Wayland 2019) and co-editor with Judith Suissa of *Critical Philosophy of Race and Education* (Routledge, 2019). Darren has been a teacher in primary schools, a teaching fellow at university and organised informal educational groups for young people and adults. He has led courses in 'Philosophy for Children' for teachers and teacher-educators and is currently completing a PhD on the politics of philosophical inquiry with children. Darren tweets at @rapclassroom